The KIDFUN®
Activity Book

The
KIDFUN®
Activity
Book

New Expanded Edition
For Ages 2½ to 8

SHARLA FELDSCHER
and
SUSAN LIEBERMAN

HarperPerennial

A Division of HarperCollinsPublishers

HarperCollins books may be purchased for educational, business, or
sales promotional use. For information, please write: Special Mar-
kets Department, HarperCollins Publishers, Inc., 10 East 53rd Street,
New York, NY 10022.

KIDFUN is a registered trademark of Sharla Feldscher.

FIRST EDITION

Feldscher, Sharla.
   The KIDFUN activity book / Sharla Feldscher and Susan Lieber-
man. —New expanded ed., lst ed.
        p. cm.
   "For ages 2-1/2 to 8."
   Includes Index.
   ISBN 0-06-273327-3
   1. Creative activities and seat work. 2. Family recreation. I.
Lieberman, Susan Abel. II. Title
GV1203.F367   1995
649'.51—dc20   94-24031

95 96 97 98 99 ◆/RRD 10 9 8 7 6 5 4 3 2 1

Of course KIDFUN® deserves to be dedicated to our own kids, Amy and Hope Feldscher and Seth and Jonathan Lieberman and our husbands, Barry and Michael. They have been wonderful partners-in-fun. But our most heartfelt impulse is to honor our own parents. Sharla wishes all little girls could have a father as wonderful as Irwin Stupine. Susan wishes all grown up parents could have a mother as supportive and generous as Ruth Abel Perrin.

Contents

Acknowledgments

Going from idea to book is a complicated process. Without the help of Maron Waxman, Rob and Joshua Kaplan, Barrie Van Dyck and Anne Langtry, we doubt the process would have made it to the end. Without insights from Cathy Engel, Meredith Young, Janet Mizopalko, Dr. Rhonda Clements, Miriam Edelman and the many families, teachers and kids who shared their ideas with us, it certainly would have happened less well. Sharla is indebted to all the Feldschers— Bobbi, Alan, Bryan, Jeannie, Erica, Cara, Sherri, Gene, Jeffrey and Neil and the Stupines and her extended family—Daddy and Ruth, Barry, Susan, Erika, Jeffrey, Lorraine and Bernie Rosenberg, Harvey, Maddy and Julie Rovinsky, the Heisens, Zaremboks and Kleinbergs—for providing a real life understanding of how much fun family can be. To Francyn Sacks, Bonnie Kaye, Jayne Zeldin and Harriet Rovner goes rousing thanks for enthusiasm, wisdom and years of friendship.

Sharla has had the fortunate and enriching experience of being associated with Sesame Place, the Anheuser-Busch Theme Park created with Children's Television Workshop, where children and their families laugh, play and learn in a most stimulating and enriching environment.

Susan owes a thank you to the SUPER SUMMERS project for allowing her time away from writing about activities for teenagers to focus once again on KID-FUN®.

Introduction

UNEXPECTED OPPORTUNITIES FOR FUN

Young children are fascinating, exciting, and joyful adventurers, eager to learn about the world. If they seem in constant motion, getting into everything, never still for more than a moment, it is because everything in their surroundings is an endless source of interest and delight. They have a wide-eyed curiosity about life, and they are ready to absorb it all.

But what they want most is to share life's experiences with others, especially the people they love. In today's fast-paced society with two-career families, single parents, community responsibilities, and consuming domestic chores, many adults have very little structured time for play. Yet our lives are full of opportunities, *unexpected opportunities*, for teaching, loving, and sharing with our children.

The most routine daily activities—driving in a car, waiting in line at the bank, bathing a toddler—are ideal times to interact happily with our children. A brief bit of laughter or a fanciful flight of imagination can turn a routine errand into a bright moment for our child and a happy memory for us.

The KIDFUN® Activity Book is a handbook for busy adults, a guide to joy, filled with hundreds of simple suggestions for making everyday events pleasurable times. Its intention is to help you focus on how to use the unexpected or routine moments in each day to create moments of pleasure and learning. Here is a typical example: You're stuck in traffic, eager to stop at the grocery store, pick up some food, and cook dinner before an evening meeting. The kids are getting restless, and you're getting hungry and irritated.

But the traffic isn't moving, so you try a KIDFUN game, such as "Talk Like Me." You and your kids recite a familiar nursery rhyme—perhaps "Mary Had a Little Lamb"—in a series of styles: Try it high-pitched, then low. Accent every third syllable or run through it as fast as you can. Recite it as a love poem, with a heavy French accent, and then with a drawl. Odds are you will end up giggling at your silliness and trade a little of the irritation for a moment of fun.

This book is about shaping such moments. It gives parents, grandparents, friends, and caretakers a repertoire of good ideas that fit the pace of busy lives. No matter how much chaos the day brings, there is usually a moment for fun, and fun makes for much better memories.

Since we completed the first version of *The KIDFUN® Activity Book* in 1990, the pace of daily life seems to have revved up another gear. "Busy," "tired," and "stressed" are three of the most popular answers to "How are you?" Parents face a difficult challenge—juggling all the pieces of their lives. This book recognizes both the busy side of life and the deep-seated desire of parents to raise happy, healthy children and have pleasure doing it. The message here is not change your life, but make the most out of the time you have with your children.

The young child, two and a half to eight, is the focus of these KIDFUN activities, but many are easily adaptable to older grade school children. Young children are eager to spend time with the people they love, even if only for a few minutes. See their imaginative efforts at seizing your attention as expressions of love. Enjoy that love and that uncomplicated pleasure in your attention and affection. It won't last long. We know. Our babies are now grown-up and they, like us, are busy. In adolescence, your children may be willing to go out with you only "if no one will see us!" It is you who may be waiting around for a bit of "quality time" from them. Their friends come first, which is just as it should be, but we find we miss their company.

Value the time you have now—while your children are young. Make no mistake. The responsibility of raising small children is not forever. Neither is the unconditional love of young children. Don't lose sight of all the pleasure it can bring you. Don't be too busy to enjoy what is very special and very short.

QUICK AND EASY ACTIVITIES

The KIDFUN® Activity Book has been written for all people who care for a young child. Parents, grandparents, baby-sitters, siblings, and teachers can use these simple suggestions, which are easy to do with material already at hand. The activities can be played with children, and they can be played by children on their own.

There is a twofold purpose to *The KIDFUN® Activity Book*. First, it offers a gold mine of activities for every occasion—for routine times and special times, quiet times and noisy times, indoors and outdoors, city and country, all seasons, all hours. In this edition, we have added over 150 new activities. These ideas are organized to reflect the ways many of us divide our time with children and to address the typical everyday events with which we regularly cope: driving in the car, waiting at restaurants, standing in line at the deli counter, giving the kids a bath, and putting them to sleep at night. There are suggestions for days when kids are feeling "under the weather" or when bad weather itself brings rainy-day doldrums or hot-day tantrums. And there are, crucially, tips for what to do with children who join you at the office and who are reluctant to join you in chores at home.

The second purpose is to inspire adults to enrich the time they and their children spend together, to seize the moment! *The KIDFUN® Activity Book* activities offer educational experiences, psychological benefits, and, we hope, giggles, wonder, and satisfaction for all. They are interactive because the whole point of this book is to expand the quality of life. We can enjoy our children, and they can enjoy us. How wonderful if a child thinks of parents and other adults as friends and later recalls the fun they had! If you share experiences and respect your child's abilities, you will be laying the groundwork for a healthy adult. While the healthy development of the child is an underlying thesis, we don't want to forget the health of the parent. Good times are good for kids—and good for parents, too.

Most of the activities are simple, short, and direct. The adults just throw the switch and set the child's mind in motion. For example, when sitting in the doctor's waiting room, do a little "invisible writing." Print a letter or draw a simple object on your child's arm or leg and ask her to guess what it is. Let her try it with you. While passing the time, you will be making the most of a trying, apprehensive situation. Your child will appreciate the distraction and the fact that you are giving her your attention when she needs it.

READ THIS LIKE A RECIPE BOOK

Every parent has an arsenal of games and ideas to entertain children, and some of the things in this book may be old staples of yours. What we found as parents is that, while we had a few good ideas, we often ran out of creative juices and were frequently saved by someone else's old standby. We think of KIDFUN as sort of a giant show-and-tell for parents.

Read it like a recipe book. Find what suits you as the occasion arises. Some of the activities are for very young children. Others work better for school-age kids. Browse through the chapters and see what strikes your fancy. Go ahead and bend the corners, make notes, and/or stick in paper clips. This is your book, and you can use it however it works best for you and your child.

KIDFUN MEANS LEARNING THROUGH PLAY

Although the educational advantages of every activity are not always stated, most activities are aimed at developing skills important to young children: Observation, discrimination, imagination, curiosity, and expression contribute to a successful school experience. That's what the term "KIDFUN" really means. When Sharla was a kindergarten teacher, she realized she could teach students anything if they were having a good time. "Education was very important in my classroom, but laughter and interaction and involvement is what people saw. My students thought they were playing. They never suspected they were being educated."

Here is an example. February was the month to teach about George Washington. The children could be taught a poem to memorize *or* they could "be" George and "be" Martha and play-act their lives. There was a wonderful moment when an apprehensive supervisor walked into Sharla's noisy classroom to ask the children what they were doing. "We're marching to Valley Forge with George," they explained. "It's cold and our feet hurt, but we won't quit." What a lesson!

"Kids are for fun," Sharla's brother popped out

delightedly when he heard this story. His words stuck, and when Sharla started writing a column for the *Philadelphia Daily News*, she used his expression for the title of the column. A wise editor shortened it to KID-FUN. The message is the same: Having fun while learning is the best motivator when teaching a young child—in school and at home.

And that is what *The KIDFUN® Activity Book* is all about—a myriad of ideas that are fun for the whole family as well as educational for the child. Some of the specific skills that are developed are obvious—math and vocabulary, for example. Some are more subtle—motor, perceptual, and conceptual growth. But the child's development will soon be apparent. She will develop a greater awareness of her environment and will increase her skills of concentration and independence.

Children benefit from an adult's input. Adults can name and explain "mysteries" and call attention to missed items. For example, when your child looks at a leaf, you can call attention to the veins, the shape and the size, and how different the leaf feels on each side. Keep pointing out small differences and encourage her to look for details. A young child's awareness will be increased when you help her notice details in her surroundings.

Awareness is important to mental growth, and a curious child can easily be encouraged to observe carefully and to use the clues in the environment. The tiniest, seemingly least important clues can lead in many directions. For example, imagine a picture of a house with trees in the background and a child sitting on the porch. Ask each other questions about the picture: Is it an old house? Do many people live in it? What time of year is it? What time of day? What is the child waiting for? Who is in the house? How long has the child been sitting there? Use your skills of observation and imagination to answer these questions, and enjoy the fun of being supersleuths.

Young children vary considerably in their language development. Some little children talk and talk and never seem to stop. Others are quiet. Too often, in adult-child relationships the adult does most of the talking. But it is very important to listen to the child and draw him out. What fascinating, innocent, and uncontrived statements come from our children! Their fresh and uncontaminated perceptions can restore our own sense of wonder and discovery. A discussion with a child can be a lot of fun, and important insights can be gained about the child's perception of the world.

Another wonderful activity for learning is creative dramatics or role-playing. In this safe medium a child can experiment with many different aspects of life and prepare for new experiences and roles. He can be a tree, a doctor, an elephant, a giant, an astronaut. Such role-playing broadens the mind and builds empathy, imagination, and understanding. The child is active and involved, using physical and mental energy creatively.

All children become restless at times. You can usually see it coming. In our families, we talk about heading into a downward spiral. If nothing happens to stop it, it can lead to a spell of crankiness or temper. When your child is fidgety, try, for example, to distract him with some form of creative dramatics. It does not take elaborate preparation or materials. Try this: Hold up a rubber band, wiggle it, throw it in the air, stretch it, and let it pop. Then ask the child to imitate the rubber band's motion. He will love to wiggle, jump in the air, stretch his body, and then fall to the ground like a rubber band popping. He can pretend to be a bouncing ball, clothes spinning in a washing machine, a jack-in-the-box. Encourage him to think of other objects to dramatize. He'll be putting his mind to work and using some of that restless energy in a very positive way.

Many activities in this book give your child opportunities to develop judgmental skills—judging the weight of an object, making size comparisons, defining the use of an object, relating cause and effect, guessing motives and outcomes. Children enjoy being a living scale. Your child stands with both hands outstretched as different objects are placed in each hand. When he lowers the hand that has the heavier object, he is making judgments and forming concepts. Sometimes he can guess in advance which of the two objects is heavier; then he can see if he is right. Ask him how he knew. Perhaps a real scale can be used later to let him check out his guesses.

The young child is totally involved with the sensory aspects of his world. He loves to explore surroundings by feeling, seeing, tasting, smelling, and shaking things. Simple games can reinforce sensory and perceptual skills. For example, blindfold your child and let him feel different objects and identify them. You can also play a noise game. Make a sound in another room and have your child guess what made the noise. He can test you, too.

You will find activities in this book that develop number, letter, and shape recognition. For example, your child can go on a treasure hunt, looking for a magnetic letter that was hidden in a room. He can use popsicle sticks to form numbers and shapes, jump on a number line taped to the floor, or pick out a particular letter on billboards. To him it is a game, but much casual learning takes place through such play. Teachers call it "reading readiness," but if you treat it as a game and don't worry about mistakes, your child will call it fun.

As the child becomes familiar with these games and activities, he will play them over and over, making variations of his own and adding more details. For example, in the memory game "What's Missing?" small objects are placed on a tray. They are removed after a few minutes, and the players try to remember all that was there. Preschoolers can do this with four or five objects. Older children may be more challenged by eight or nine. Make the games more challenging as the child grows.

EVERY CHILD IS AN ARTIST

Art activities appear in many guises in these chapters, since art is important in the development of a young child's mind. Art offers children a powerful and satisfying way to communicate what they know about the world. Children give us important information about themselves and their perceptions with their choices of materials and subjects. Their words are in that drawing. It is important communication, once we learn the language.

Adults are often puzzled by a page of squiggles or an abstract landscape. They don't know what the drawing represents, and if they ask "What is it?" the artist is disappointed. To avoid this, simply say, "How nice! Tell me about it." This gives the child room to respond in any way he wants and, incidentally, to develop descriptive language. If an adult keeps asking for identification, the child may try too hard to draw only concrete things and may lose his creativity and enjoyment of art for itself. This can lead to frustration and artistic inhibition.

Find something to praise; appreciate the effort. Discuss the technique the child used—the colors, the straight or curvy lines, and the way the drawing fills the paper.

SIMPLE GIMMICKS

Simple gimmicks keep our kids from losing interest. While playing a game, add variety by asking your child to be the "judge" who must decide on a winner or to time the activity or to try it with one hand on top of his head. Kids need gimmicks; we all need gimmicks. Television commercials use them to interest consumers in products; advertisers use them on billboards. Their purpose is to capture our attention and to arouse our curiosity. When telling your child to pretend he is a giant and take seven giant steps, he is first being a giant, but he is also using math and language skills. The "giant" gimmick has grabbed his attention.

If your child is to be interested and involved, she must be active. Sitting back and watching others is never as enjoyable or instructional as actually participating. If your child is bored, challenge her to stand up and jump fifty times. Count with her while she jumps. Clap your hands to keep the pace steady. Join in and then collapse on the floor together! Another simple gimmick to rouse your child from a dull moment is to speak in whispers or to speak high, low, fast, or slow. Invite your child to invent a different manner of speaking too. Learning is fun, especially when the learner is an active, interested participant.

THE JOY OF LEARNING

Remember, the ideas contained in this book are only suggestions. Don't force them. They are geared to young children with short attention spans, and they are informal activities. Their primary goal is to occupy your child joyously, playfully, creatively. The learning of skills should happen unobtrusively. If your child enjoys the activity, his enthusiasm for learning will increase. However, if too much is offered to a child who is not ready, he will not be eager to continue. Some children are not ready to learn when their parents think they should be. This does not mean your child is slow or a reluctant learner. Readiness comes at different times to different children. Often your child is busy learning many other things, which are to him more interesting or more important. When your children show up on their wedding day, no one will know—or care—what month they learned to read or count by threes or whether they were the first or the last on the block to tie their shoes.

The joy of learning can be blended with the joy of giving, as you'll see at the end of the book in the chapter called "KIDFUN Gifts." The best gifts you can give a child are ones that encourage creativity. Homemade kits filled with unexpected items can lead to loads of fun and, incidentally, lots of learning. A mini business case with stamps and stamping pads, old checks, business cards, order pads, and pens will fill the imagination of a youngster and be a very welcome gift. A wrapped carton with old but fanciful hats, a cloth cape, and white gloves can turn a typical toddler into a dramatic darling who will relish this gift and use it repeatedly. Your gift has turned the key on his imaginative powers.

KIDFUN IS FOR ALL FAMILIES

We hope that all families will seize those unexpected opportunities and build a foundation of love and sharing and fun that will be a source of joy to last a lifetime. Take advantage of those opportunities that draw you and your child together and find the energy, somehow, to say to your child, "Okay, let's play a game." When initiating an idea from this book, offer it as a suggestion, never as a command. If things don't work, let go! But when they do, you are likely to trip into an unexpected insight, a peal of laughter for both of you, a spur-of-the-moment special conversation, or a burst of learning for your child. The result, we hope, will be a happier now and a more loving tomorrow.

STOCK TIP

KIDFUN activities are designed to be easy and simple. Most require only a child, an adult and the desire to have fun. Some, however, use supplies. Many of these—buttons or rubber bands, crayons or pillows— you will already have on hand. However, for your convenience, you will find a shopping list at the end of the book of "ingredients" used in KIDFUN activities. You may want to stock up and keep a KIDFUN box tucked away for those days when something new is what you want to do.

1

Traveling Fun, Especially in the Car

F or young children, car rides and plane rides mean a restriction of movement. Since a small child's natural state is to be in motion, being confined to a small place and instructed to "stay put" can be hard. Adults must be particularly ingenious in engaging children's minds when their bodies are restricted by necessary safety belts.

Keep a goodies bag in the car to amuse your child during trips. It might include some small stuffed animals, a finger puppet, a toy airplane, a prism (which works well with older children), and a cassette player with a few story or song tapes. Add an occasional surprise—a magic slate board or a small chalkboard or some adventure characters—to keep the bag interesting. For older children, think about simple magic tricks.

Children frequently get hungry during long car rides. Head off whines and tantrums by keeping a supply of food on hand. Instead of candy, consider an emergency rations bag with small boxes of raisins, little sealed packets of cheese and crackers, and small boxes of cereal.

Riding in the car—or in buses, boats, trains, and planes—offers a wonderful opportunity to engage your child—and yourself—in observing the surroundings. Make them aware of the details around them, especially the little things that are easily missed: the color of smoke against the sky, the pattern of telephone wires or birds perched on poles, the length of the shadows on a winter day. Talk about what you see. Make up stories about the people you pass in other cars or on the streets.

When your child, or you, has lost interest in looking at the passing scene, engage him in games that can be played buckled up in a seat. The suggestions here are just a start. Improvise others, and as your child's awareness grows, travel times will begin to seem shorter.

Tape Talk

Take a tape recorder and a blank tape with you in the car. Let your child make a story tape. Begin the story by giving him a setting like the woods or the beach. Choose the characters who will start the story or have your child decide who the characters are. For example, you could say, "One day as I walked in the woods, I saw a great, big, furry. . . ." Then, let your child continue. Turn on the recorder and let your child begin talking. When he comes to a halt, turn off the recorder and offer a question, based on the story he has taped so far. Periodically, let the storyteller rewind the tape and listen to the tale-in-progress. If there are several children in the car, all may take turns talking into the tape recorder. You may want to set some time limits so waiting for a turn does not become too frustrating.

A story can continue over many trips, or a new story can start over the old one. Some children like making the tape and then lose interest. Others will enjoy hearing their stories played at bedtime or some other quiet time.

Wave if You're Famous

This idea will create great excitement for all ages as it did for the Schlessinger family. You can fill the car with laughter with one simple sign. On shirt cardboard or a large piece of paper, write in large block letters: WAVE IF YOU'RE FAMOUS. Let your children hold the sign up to a window and enjoy the fun other people have responding.

First Letter

If you and "Melissa" are riding together in the car, help her think up words that begin with the first letter of her name—M. Give lots of clues. For example, you can say, "Okay, Melissa, what is daddy? He is not a woman, he is a. . . ." Or, "Inside the hood of this car is an M word that makes the car run. It is a. . . ." Ask her, "Who delivers the mail? What comes out in the sky at night? What do you pour over your cereal?"

When you have exhausted M, you can use G for Great Kid, F for Funny Person, L for Love you lots, and so on.

Signs of the Times

Even pre-readers can be entertained by billboards. Ask your child to watch the billboards as you pass and try to guess the products being shown. Some children like to sing commercials from television that match the products advertised. Talk about how many of the billboard products your child has used that week and how many your family has used. Think generically—

bread counts even if it isn't the brand being advertised.

Children who are learning letters can find the letters
of the alphabet in sequence from signs along the road.
Even older children seem to get caught up in the challenge of how fast they can drive through the alphabet.
And once a child begins to read, billboards are a great
way for him to show off letter, sound, and word recognition.

Two Word Words

Words are a generous gift for children. The richer
their vocabulary, the more they will be able to understand complicated emotions and ideas. The confines of
the car are a perfect place for having fun with words.

One game to help build vocabulary is to look for
two-word words. Of course, you will probably see a
bill-board, an *auto-mobile* and a *super-market*. Maybe
you'll see an *air-plane*, a *play-ground*, a *ball-field*, a *grave-
yard*, a *mail-man* by a *mail-box* or a *news-paper* in a *news-
stand*.

If you run out of two-word words, you can talk
about how words get linked so, in fact, we use them as
one word. Maybe you will pass a *parking lot*, a *school
house*, a *grocery store* or an *apartment house*. You and
your child can be on the look out for *fire-men* and *fire
trucks*, *gas stations*, *fast food* and corners where you
must *slow down* in case there is a *speed trap*.

For younger children, make it simpler and do
CHOPPY TALK. Accent every syllable of words. Get
your child to mimic you and then, together, count the
syllables. He will learn that *au-to-mo-bile* has more of
those silly syllables than *air-plane* or *roc-ket*.

Remember Stories

Pick a recent event that you and your child shared—maybe a visit to a favorite aunt or a birthday party or a shopping spree—and take turns remembering what you saw and did. Your child might say, "When we went to Aunt Jayne's house, I played with Craig and Todd's trains." You may add, "And Aunt Jayne made French toast," and your son remembers, "And you spilled the syrup on your blouse."

Take turns remembering more and more details until no one can think of anything else to add, then choose a different past experience.

_____ GLOOM STRATEGY _____

If your child wants to talk about an experience that was unpleasant, ask him what he would have liked to have done to change such a time from bad to good.

Stick to events that are recent. Avoid going too far back in the past unless it was a really memorable occasion for your child as well as you. Don't chastise your child for forgetting events you think are important. You can be sure that someday he will vividly remember ones you will have forgotten.

Guess My Song

Choose a song that you are sure your child knows and hum the first line. If your child recognizes the song, he sings the next line. If he doesn't guess, keep humming the song until he remembers. He sings the words as soon as he knows the song you have chosen. Then it is his turn to hum a song for you to guess.

What Do I See?

Encourage your child to look, really look, at what you are driving past. Ask him to help you notice what is happening in the towns and the landscape you pass. Call out objects—odd objects like rooftop colors, screws on telephone poles, and sneakers dangling on wires—and ask questions like these:

What color are most of the houses? Can you find the most unusual colors? What do you like best?

How many rooftops can you find that are green? How many are brown?

Let's count the kids on the block. Are there more young people or old?

Look at the trees. Are they the same? What's different?

How many churches or bars or cows or fire stations or libraries or drugstores can you count? (One category at a time of course.)

With older children, you might ask "research questions":

From what you see on the road, what do you think is important when buying cars?

How do highway designers try to protect houses and businesses from noise?

How are buildings here different from where Grandma lives?

Instant Sketch

Encourage your child to be an artist and draw some pictures of what he sees from the car window. Provide a pad of paper and a pencil. If it's a long trip, add some colored pencils, markers, or crayons. Just as you always keep a spare tire, it is a good idea to keep a tablet and a box of colored pencils in the car (unless your child is prone to getting car sick).

TRAVELERS' TIP

Keep a large plastic cookie sheet in the trunk of the car. When your child wants to write or draw on a trip, the tray makes a practical lap board for the creative artist.

If your child is a thorough sort and likes working intensely on one project, ask about details in the picture. Are there trees around the building? Are there clouds in the sky? What kinds of people are in the picture? But if your child is less patient and likes to keep moving, talk about capturing several pictures from the trip. Ask your child to make sure he draws a picture of buildings, one of cars, one of people, and one of the trees and sky.

And if your child is more apt to look into his own imagination, ask your back-seat artist to capture some pictures of that as well.

HURRY ALERT

When you arrive at your destination, even if the traffic was heavy and you are running late, don't forget to take a minute to look at the pictures and put them carefully on the seat for closer inspection later.

Car Ride Chorus

Since you are riding in your chariot, do what the song says and "swing low." Take turns choosing a popular song for all to sing together. Some family favorites are: "I've Been Working on the Railroad," "You're a Grand Old Flag," "This Old Man," "Take Me Out to the Ball Game," "Jingle Bells," "I've Got Six Pence." If you have lots of people in the car (including a few adults), you might want to divide into two or three groups and sing simple rounds like "Row, Row, Row Your Boat."

The car is a perfect place to teach children songs from your childhood—or have them teach you songs they have learned at school. If you like Broadway or movie musicals, play tapes of them and learn the words together. Try themes from favorite television shows or commercials. Share the music *you* like with your child, and learn his favorites too.

MUSIC LOVERS' MESSAGE

If you have a cassette player in the car, buy tapes of children's songs or your favorite folk songs and practice singing them with and then without the tape. Or bring blank tapes and record your own family chorus.

Talk Like Me

It is amazing what dramatic effects you can get simply by changing your speaking style. A child can develop sound-discrimination skills by playing with his voice in any number of ways.

Try it like this. Count, unroll the alphabet, or recite a nursery rhyme in your normal manner. Now change your speech: Talk very fast or slow, use a high-pitched voice and then a deep bass voice; break everything up into choppy syllables, or put an accent on every third word, and so on. Challenge your child to mimic you exactly as he heard you.

Most children love this kind of word play, and they learn much about words and speech by playing with their voices. For instance, you can turn "Mary Had a Little Lamb" into a love poem, a mystery, or a proclamation simply by varying your speech pattern. Try reciting it the way you think a Frenchman or a German or a Chinese or a southerner might.

Tune Turning

Try turning some of your favorite tunes into your own family songs. If you are on your way to Aunt Bonnie's for example, the aunt with a fat and furry cat named Delilah, you can borrow the tune to "Old MacDonald Had a Farm" and sing "Old Delilah had some stripes, itch y itch y o. And on her stripes she has some fleas, itch y itch y o..."

Try all sorts of songs and all sorts of word changes to make the songs your own. A few are likely to strike you all as funny and may become family jokes. If you really like one of your inventions, tape it so you can remember.

A Sorry Sight

Look out the window and scan the environment with a critical eye. Each time one of you spots something that spoils the beauty or is bad for our health, announce "Pollution!" and tell what it is. It may be trash littering the street, exhaust fumes from a truck or car, or smoke from a factory. Discuss what causes pollution. Compare and rate the various areas you drive through.

If you feel strongly that all of us must help care for our environment, you may want to stop the car occasionally for a little pickup so a nice place will look more beautiful.

Taxonomy

Choose a category. Tell everyone in the car to watch out the windows for one thing. You might choose dogs, trees, flowers, traffic signs, trucks, public buildings, and so on.

Each time one of you sees something in the chosen category, he calls it out and points to it. Everyone tries to identify the specific species. If your category is dogs, is the dog you are seeing a poodle, a shepherd, or a mongrel? If the category is buildings, have you spotted a library, a post office, a hospital, or a school?

This game is best played when older children or more than one adult are in the car or when there is very little traffic. You don't want to be scrutinizing the breed of a particular dog or trying to read the building sign while the car in front of you is stopping short.

For variation, someone in the car can write the category at the top of a piece of paper and your child can draw a picture beneath it. Then let your child make a mark for each item you spot. When you change categories, have your child draw a new picture and mark the items in this category. By the end of the trip, you will have a record of the number of different kinds of things you observed on your way.

Various trips may go down in family memory as "the cow trip" or "the church ride."

Echo

Make a sound and repeat it a number of times. You can tap the car window, click your tongue, repeat a syllable (lalalalala), tap your foot, and so forth. Tell your child to listen carefully and count how many times you make the sound. Then he must echo you, repeating the sound just as you made it. Now it is your child's turn to make a sound while you count and repeat. Be patient if he does not count or repeat just right. This is not a test; this is for fun, and the more you practice, the better his sound discrimination will become.

Grandfather's Chest

This is a funny game that builds memory and concentration. The first person starts by chanting, "I went to the attic and found. . . ." He can name anything he likes. It can be a real object or an imaginative one. For example, "I went to the attic and found a purple dog with yellow stripes" (or a submarine floating upside down, a gold pocket watch, three Martians, a one-armed doll).

The second person repeats the chant: "I went to the attic and found. . . ." He must name the object the first person found and then add another object of his own choosing as part of an ongoing story. The game continues in this way, with each person repeating everything already named plus one additional item. See how many you can remember in sequence by counting them when the game falls apart.

Another way to share a "grandfather's tale" is to mention items alphabetically. For example, when Jane went to the attic she found an *a*lligator, but I found a *bat.*" Then the next person repeats the *a* word and *b* word but adds a *c* word.

─────────────── TRAVEL TIP ───────────────

Make up your own memory builders and name objects in a specific category that get repeated as each new one is added. Make it imaginative. For example, "I went to a crazy zoo and I saw a tiny red elephant, a snake wearing bedroom slippers, a short giraffe," and so on and so on.

T Talk

Take turns choosing a letter. You and your child look out the window, calling out anything that begins with that letter. If your child is just learning letter sounds, give him helpful hints.

If an older child is in the car, he can act as a recorder and list the words called out. Later, young children may want to draw pictures of some of the things they saw.

Try starting with the letter "T" and be alert for: trucks, tricycles, trains, trees, trunks, tires, tanks, telephones, and tables.

Schoolchildren may spot toes and tinfoil and teeth, taxis and tubes and tunnels.

If "T Talk" takes off, there are tails, trails, tags, trailers, tattoos, terraces, tents, temples, taverns, telescopes, telegraph poles, teams, timepieces, thumbs, tomatoes, tissues, traffic, tar, and triangles to be spotted.

And if older children want to play, tell them all the easy words are off limits for them. They must be especially clever and come up with thighs, togetherness, thinness, titles, textbooks, tiles, tops, turns, tongues, and Toyotas.

Start out looking for ten T's. Then try to beat your own record. Then try, oh, maybe, S or B or. . . .

Rhyme Time

Start with a simple one-syllable word such as "cat," and take turns supplying rhyming words that belong in the same word family: for example, bat, hat, fat, mat, rat, pat, slat, spat. Then try to put some of these words together in a silly story, such as "One, two, three, I see a bee. Don't bite me. Fly into that tree."

Then see what happens to your story when you combine the same words in a new way: "I sat in a tree. Up came a bee. He said don't bite me. I want to fly away free." Remember to give your child a chance. Even grown-ups with large vocabularies find themselves challenged to see how many silly stories they can make out of these common words.

Guess What It Is

Maybe you played this simple game with your parents—and they with their parents. Tell your child you are thinking of an object and he must guess it. Give him one clue. If he doesn't guess correctly, give him another clue. Continue with clues and guesses until he names the object. Your clues should describe what the object looks like or what it is used for. For example, if you are thinking of the steering wheel, clue number one might be: "It is round." Clue two: "It helps send the car in the right direction." Clue three: "The driver must touch it." Clue four: "I need to hold it when I am driving."

Make your clues easy and obvious at first so that your child can quickly guess. When he gets to be good at the game, you can make the clues more subtle and provide obvious clues only when needed.

Take turns guessing and giving clues.

From Here to There

When your child is impatient to cover the distance, set him to counting particular objects from here to there. She might count how many stoplights or stop signs or gas stations there are from home to the highway ramp or from school to the supermarket.

Or challenge her to see how high the two of you can count before reaching the next light or how many different songs you can sing before the next toll booth.

Making Commercials

Parents may wish for fewer commercials on children's television, but kids often see them as part of the entertainment. Our friend Seth, for example, knows scads of jingles by heart and likes to sing them, sometimes mimicking the voices on TV.

Try naming a product while you are driving (maybe inspired by the billboards)—milk or cereal or toilet paper—and see if you and your child can sing a jingle or say a rhyme from advertising for that product. If you can't—or even if you can—make up your own. Some kids we know are waiting for Campbell's Soup to buy their jingle:

Want to eat something funky?
Try our soup that's real chunky.
Use a spoon or just zoop
And you'll like Campbell's Soup.

This activity can be adapted readily to kids of every age.

I'm Famous

This is a variation on that old reliable "Twenty Questions," except all the questions describe a famous person. One person says, "I'm thinking of somebody famous. Guess who I am." Other people ask questions describing that person, but the answers may be only yes or no. For example, you cannot ask "What movie were you in last year?" Only "Were you in a movie last year?" "Was it funny?" "Was it serious?" and so on.

Traditionally, you have only twenty questions to guess the person, but the game can be played so that after twenty questions, the "famous person" must give three clues and you have twenty more questions—or whatever other rules you want to devise—in which to guess.

License Plates

No matter what country you visit, you are likely to find kids playing games with the number and letter patterns on car license plates. Try some of these for variety:

- Doubles and triples—look for letters and numbers that are duplicated in the plate.

- States—see how many different states you can spot on the plates.

- Vanity plates—look for the plates that spell out a message and decide which you think is the funniest and what message people mean to send.

- Twenty-one—look for plates with numbers that add up to twenty-one or any other number combination you want.

- Alphabet—recite the alphabet in order by finding the letters in license plates.

Spell Check

While younger children are looking out for license plates, you can develop the spelling powers of older children with this activity. One person mentions a word, and the next person follows with a word that begins with the last letter of the word just mentioned. For example, "Kite" could be followed by "elephant" by "touch" by "horse." Play this game against the clock. Challenge your crew to say five words in sixty seconds or ten words in two minutes. Then see if you can go faster.

Going Elsewhere

Pretend with your child that, instead of going to the bank or the store, you are going Elsewhere. Decide where you want to go, what you need to take with you, and what you will do when you get there. Pack your Elsewhere suitcase and plan your Elsewhere adventure. Share in describing the details of how you are traveling and what you will find once you get there.

Sometimes driving in heavy traffic demands all of your concentration; you need quiet. Keep a two- or three-minute egg timer in the car. When the traffic, or your mind, hits overload, hand your child the timer and ask for quiet time out while the sand flows down. If necessary, have him turn it over and wait for the sand to flow down again.

Story Tape

Even though the car is a good place to interact with your child, there may be times when road and traffic conditions are so demanding that you must focus all your attention on driving. You need your child to sit quietly while you concentrate on the driving.

For times like these, give your child a cassette player with earphones. Use story tapes you have made, bought, or borrowed from the library to engross your child. Make sure, however, to find time later to talk with your child about the story.

Car Cooking

If you are on your way home to lunch or dinner and the drive is long, you and your child might work up an appetite by car cooking. Decide what you would like to eat—say your child decides it should be pizza. Suggest that you and he cook imagination pizza in the car.

Ask him what you would have to do first. If he tells you it is throw the dough in the air, talk about how you get the dough. Talk about what goes into tomato paste and how to grind cheese and dry herbs.

_____ MENU MINDER _____

Be kind to your taste buds. Don't make imaginary pizza
the day you plan on serving broccoli and fish for dinner. Both you and child are going to be tasting that
pizza.

If your child gets interested in car cooking, follow it
up by making the real thing at home, remembering
what you discussed in the car. Or ask your babysitter
to invite your child to cook something together.

Alpha What

When your child is gearing up to read and can tell
the difference between different alphabet sounds, he
may be ready for this. This is fun for grown-ups, too,
and older kids will happily jump in and help the little
ones. Make it a team effort.

Pick a category—like animals or people you know,
articles of clothing or places to go. Then go through the
alphabet naming things in your category in alphabeti-
cal order—ant, baboon, crab, dog. . . . If young children need help, go ahead and help them. The intent is
simply to engage the two of you and, along the way,
learn sounds and words.

If older children are in the car, you can play this as a
two tier game. First the younger child thinks of ant,
than the older child must name another "A" animal—
like aardvark or abalone. You can play, too or you can
be everybody's assistant. If you can't think of something in a reasonable amount of time, move on to keep
kids from getting bored.

—————— HOME REFERENCE ——————

When you get home, pick one object your little one didn't know about—aardvark, for example—and look it up in a book. Stop at one and it will be fun.

Goody Necklace

The cereal aisle at the supermarket offers more than breakfast food. It is a great source of supplies for all kinds of arts and crafts projects. For example, pick up some Cheerios. These low sugar circles are great for stringing into necklaces or bracelets. Tape the end of a long piece of string to the table and let your child make a long Cheerio necklace which you will tie closed. Then pop it in a plastic bag and save it for the very next car trip. Drop it around your child's neck and let him munch at will.

Kids' Directions

If your child is trying to learn right and left, help him by taking five minutes in the car for a game of Directions—but do this in a quiet subdivision, not the middle of busy traffic. Let him direct your driving with left and right instructions. If he tells you to turn left, do it while he holds up his left hand for a second. You can raise your left hand too, and so, "Okay, the car is heading left." If he tells you to turn right and there is no right turn, just pull over and stop the car and say, "Communications failure—car cannot go ahead as instructed."

After several turns, see if he can reverse his instructions and direct you back to the starting place.

—————— SPATIAL RELATIONS ——————

Once your child knows right and left and is a bit older, you can use the car to help him develop a feel for distance by driving a quarter of a mile, a half mile, a mile and then by estimating a 100 feet, 500 feet, 1000 feet in the car.

Got It First

Get the kids to make up travel rules. When you see a pizza place, for example, say "CHEESE." When you cross a railroad track, lift both feet. And if you see a dog, bark. The object is to be the first person in the car to get it right. First passenger to collect ten points is the GOT IT FIRST winner for that trip. (In case of ties, each gets a point.)

Finger Puppets

It's rush hour and you and your child are about to get stuck together in traffic which is too intense for doing much but concentrating on the cars. This is for those emergency times when your child is eager to talk but you know you can't.

Before you start driving, find a magic marker—better yet, find two of different colors. Make faces on your child's fingers—a smiley face, a frowning face, an O-pen mouthed face. Make three faces on one hand and two faces on the other.

Now start driving and ask your child to name each face and introduce one to another. Ask him if he can tell them stories, sing them songs and keep them entertained while you drive as quickly as you can through the traffic.

2.

Waiting Together

Time spent waiting is one of the things parents and children most often share. We may be waiting in the "short" line at the bank or at the deli counter in the food market. We may be waiting to pay a bill or buy a product or ask a question. We wait to be seated and served in restaurants, take a turn on the swings, or have the storyteller begin her story. We are in the same situation with our child, and it helps children to know that grown-ups can find waiting hard too.

Sometimes we are in an official "waiting room"— perhaps visiting the doctor or dentist—and some anxiety is attached to the waiting. Playing quiet, creative games that distract a child in this situation creates a special sense of appreciation and can lead to one of those tender moments when our children let us know we are especially important and helpful.

Although waiting is a daily occurrence, it is contrary to the natural make-up of a young child, who has not yet mastered the art of being patient. We may feel as impatient as our children. We may also feel guilty for having them wait in line with us, feel anxious to get home to start dinner, or worry about being late for the next activity. Waiting games make the time pass more quickly for both the child and for us.

Since we spend so much time each week waiting, it helps to think of these minutes not as wasted time but play time in which we can steal a bit of fun with our children. In a hustle-bustle world, consider waiting time as an unscheduled opportunity.

Be prepared. Keep a bag of assorted materials handy to grab on your way out the door that will help your child stay occupied while you wait. A small notebook and colored pencils, a few match-box cars, a good book for reading all help. And use the space around you as the best ingredient for play. The walls, the furniture, the people nearby can lead to all sorts of guessing game activities that build your child's skills and make the wait more fun.

Try the activities in "Waiting Together" and create your own. Perhaps they will help you recall games you played when you were a waiting child.

Name Three

This is a simple classification game. You or your child picks a category—ice cream flavors, cars, animals, states, ways to travel, disgusting habits, TV programs—and says "Name three (category)." If this is just you and your child, trade off choosing the category and asking each other. If several kids are present, you might give each child a different category to think about in turn. Or the kids can take turns. One asks and the next person answers. Then, as soon as that person names three, she asks the next person.

NIM

This game is especially good for restaurants. It is an elimination game that exercises abstract reasoning powers and works for all ages but the very young.

Line up sixteen sugar packets (or pieces of paper if you like), four rows down and four rows across. Each person takes a turn removing any number of packets from one horizontal row at a time. The object is to avoid picking up the last remaining packet.

NIM can also be played with a grid drawn on paper. Instead of lining up sugar packets, draw your short lines in each row of the grid. Take turns crossing off lines until one is remaining. Try using the back of a paper place mat or paper napkin.

Monster Moments

Now, you might tell your child, is a Monster Moment. Stuck with nothing to do but wait, draw some monsters. Let your child choose any shape—triangle, circle, square (and for older kids, hexagon, octagon, parallelogram. . .).

For example, draw a large triangle in the center of the paper. Now, watch it turn into a monster by adding big, sharp teeth; freaky, wild hair; giant feet; claws; pointy ears. Of course, the monster will need a name. Help your child come up with something really frightening.

You might want to take the monsters home to put in a monster book.

Best Friend Stories

If you are stuck in a waiting room with magazines, try out Best Friend Stories. Wait until a person or an animal catches your child's interest. Then ask her to imagine who he, she or it would have as a best friend.

Would this dog choose a cat, a mouse, a moose or a boy?

Make up a story about the best friend. Ask your child what they do together, what kinds of games they play, what they eat and if they fight. If your child is having a particular behavior problem—snatching toys from other kids, perhaps—you might slide in a subtle message about the best friend snatching toys and your child helping the best friend learn how to share—but let your child lead the conversation. You will learn a lot about what is on her mind.

Don't stop your child from choosing seemingly mis-matched pairs. If the elephant decides to have a mouse as a best friend, you have been handed a delicious opportunity to discuss how differences can add to a friendship, not distract from it.

_____ AD-DIVERSE-MENT _____

We think having lots of different kinds of friends is a real benefit for children. This activity is a good way to let your child know that you like the idea of her knowing different kinds of people.

Black Magic

This KIDFUN game revolves around a magician and an assistant, who plays the role of "mind reader." The mind-reading trick is simple: The secret object always follows an object that is black. Here is how to play.

The mind reader closes his eyes while the magician silently points out an object for others to see. When the mind reader opens his eyes, the magician asks him questions like this:

"Am I thinking of the salt?" The mind reader says "No."

"Am I thinking of the napkin?" "No."

"Am I thinking of the pepper?" "No."

"Am I thinking of the ketchup?" To this, the mind reader says "Yes," because it follows a black object, the pepper.

Others in the group can now pick out objects, and the magician and mind reader continue their feat until their mystical powers are discovered.

────────── WAITING TIP ──────────

If you are desperate for paper and none is available, think about the deposit slips in the back of your checkbook.

Paper, Scissors, Rock

Your grandparents probably played this game as kids, maybe even your great grandparents.

And it still works.

Two people face each other. On the count of three, each person puts one hand in front of him signifying paper (the hand is flat), scissors (the middle and index finger are pointed in the shape of a V, like scissors blades, while the other two fingers are tucked under) or rock (the hand is curved in a fist).

Because scissors cut paper, it wins over paper. Rock, which smashes scissors, wins over scissors. Paper covers rock, so it wins when the other person has rock. Begin playing with the chant, "Paper, Scissors, Rock. . . " as if we you were counting one, two, three. . . . Then each person puts his hand sign out at the same time. If both of you have the same fingers, it is a takeover. First person to score 10 points wins the round.

Connect the Dots

Make dots on a piece of paper—the back of place mats or prescription pads is good—and invite your child to connect them, making an abstract design. Next time, let her make the dots. She may think it is more fun to make the dots with her eyes closed.

See how many different patterns she can create. Your child may want to give one of these creations to the doctor when he or she is ready to see her. If she has crayons, use different colors to connect the dots.

If your child is beginning to work on numbers, try numbering the dots.

Picture Stories

Look at the pictures on the walls where you are waiting. Let your child choose one and make up a story about that picture.

If it is a picture of a person, invent his or her life's history. If it is a scene, decide who the people are just outside the picture (though they aren't shown) and what they are doing.

In this way, you will learn many things about your child's imagination and perception. If your child has trouble getting started with this activity, try telling your own stories for a while, stopping to ask your youngster for help with the details.

Common Features

The object of this game is to look for common characteristics of objects and people in the environment. It is a conversation and a counting game that stimulates awareness, observation, and discrimination.

For example, your child may notice a person wearing eyeglasses, and then everyone counts the total number of people who are wearing eyeglasses. You can look for brown shoes, blond hair, trees in artwork.

With older children, this game can be used to begin to teach the concept of percentages. Out of the next ten people, how many have blond hair? Of the cars in the parking lot, how many are black? Will that be true for the next parking lot too?

Twenty-One

The game "21" is the "Musical Chairs" of counting games, and it is perfect for waiting or traveling times. The game simply involves counting with others and eliminating the person who gets stuck with the number "twenty-one." The only rule is that players count either one number or two numbers in numerical order. For example, the first person says, "One." The next person says, "Two, three." The following person can say either "Four" or "Four, five." You keep going until someone is stuck saying "Twenty-one." This is a good thinking game for all ages. Try a little variety by counting to a bigger odd number, such as thirty-five or forty-seven or ninety-nine. The thought process is the same, but it takes longer.

Inventory

Tell your child about how businesses take inventory. Each business must keep a count of everything it owns. The shoe store owner counts the chairs and the shoes and the boots and the socks and the customers who come in each day. Ask your child to help the store owner take inventory. Suggest a category in which she can start counting. You can count things or you can count people (including the number of boys and the number of girls) or you can count events and note how many times red cars pass by.

You may want to draw a simple chart as you do your counting so you can keep track of your inventory. Perhaps the store owner would like to have it when you leave.

NUMBER CRUNCHER

When kids get older and start learning multiplication tables, take inventory by twos or threes or. . . . If there are six boxes on most shelves, can your child count the shelves and estimate how many boxes are on one wall?

Unfinished Business

Often our children have agendas that don't fit with ours. They want to tell us all about the doll corner or the newest game Peter got while we want to discuss eating peas or brushing teeth or while we are in the middle of a conversation with someone else. Young children, unlike computers, don't have very good long-term memory storage. You can't expect a child to save for two or three days what happened that morning at nursery school; if you don't listen when the message is on the screen, it may be lost forever.

Some topics do keep, however, and these are the ones you want to remember—maybe even write down—and have on hand for waiting time. *Now*, you can tell your child, *finally* we have a good time to talk about: what you want for your birthday party... why Peter cries all the time... your list for Santa... what color you would like to paint your wall... your favorite television shows... all the things you have been doing in school.

Just one note of caution: If you are waiting in a situation that has some anxiety for either you or your child, like the doctor's office, keep to pleasant subjects, not ones that can bring on a conflict.

Did You Ever, Ever, Ever?

One of the best gifts children give us is their ability to keep us in touch with nonsense. Since much of the adult world makes no sense at all, it is only fair that children get their chance too. Both you and your child will enjoy whispering this delightful nonsense rhyme:

Did you ever, ever, ever?
Did you ever, ever, ever?
Did you ever see a CAT
Eat a–(hat?)
OH! NO! We never saw a CAT eat a HAT!

One of you recites the first three lines, and the other provides the fourth line to complete the rhyme. Then you both recite the fifth line together. The words don't have to make sense. They can be as silly as you like, but they must rhyme. For example:

Did you ever see a SHOE eat some GLUE?
Did you ever see a HIPPO do a FLIPPO?
Did you ever see a FLEA sting a BEE?

――――――――――   LOONEY TUNE   ――――――――――

Turn your rhyme into a song. Select a familiar tune and add your own words, or make up your own tune.

Magazine Spotting

Even if your child can't read the magazines left in waiting rooms, they are useful entertainment. Suggest an object—flowers or cakes or cars or baseball players—for your child to count in one of the magazines. Or take two magazines and race each other to find the object—remembering, of course, that you want to fill time, not win the game. After you have found one object, see how many more of the same are in the magazine.

Tell Me More

Kids are natural storytellers. You may be delighted by your child's imagination if you draw a simple picture and ask your child to tell you what to add to the picture in order to create a story. For example, draw a birthday cake and have the child tell you who is celebrating. Keep adding details to your picture as your child elaborates. And keep asking more questions about who came to the party, what they brought, what food they ate, and so on.

Other simple things to draw, even if you are not an adept artist, are a baseball diamond, a bed, an airplane, or a ghost.

Zoomgoom Adventures

Many children have imaginary friends. Our friend Sally had an imaginary friend named Zoomgoom. Zoomgoom did not like to be bored or to wait patiently or sit still. When Sally had to wait somewhere, she and her mom or dad would imagine what Zoomgoom would do to make the wait more interesting.

Zoomgoom could make it snow in the summer and heat up in the winter. He could turn on indoor sprinklers and shower money in the supermarket and tell very funny jokes that made all the bank clerks laugh so hard they could not count their money. You and your child may wish to have an imaginary friend like Zoomgoom to liven up the waits.

Make sure you discuss with your child the difference between imagining something and actually doing it. It is important that children understand that we are not rewarded or punished for what we think but for what we do.

One Guess

Guessing games are good in all kinds of situations. Here is one version that works well when you are waiting in one place for a long time. Ask your child to pick out an object she sees in the room. You are to guess what she has picked out by asking questions about the object (or person). For example: Is it very big? Is it very small? Is it something I can hold? Is it on the wall? Is it green? Be sure the question brings a yes or no response.

You can ask as many questions as you want but you get only one guess to identify the object. Your child will tell you if you are right or wrong. Then it is your turn to pick an object and have your child ask the questions.

If you want to make the game last longer, start with very general questions and work slowly toward the specific. Your child will probably enjoy stumping you for a while.

WAITING TIP

Waiting can be a time to help your child learn how to sit quietly and peacefully. If you are waiting in a place that is not too full of noise and distraction, try talking to your child about relaxing. You might start listening very quietly to your breathing and see if you can slow it down. You might start with your feet and think about relaxing all the parts of your body. You might hold hands and see if you can feel a quiet space grow up around you. Don't expect this to come easily and don't be irritated if you fall into the spirit of this only to be interrupted by a child's question. Learning comes slowly and it comes best when there is positive reinforcement, not correction.

Wish List

Have you ever bought a lottery ticket or entered a sweepstake and found yourself imagining what you would do if you won millions? If you are in a restaurant waiting for food, a good activity for the family is to imagine how you would spend a million dollar lottery jackpot. It's just fun to dream about owning a mansion, a race horse, a yacht or an island. Share the dreams together.

--- WISH AWAY ---

If you want your child to keep sharing wishes, don't get trapped into thinking you should censor your child's wishes to make them "better." For example, if your child wishes she could spend all her money on purple sneakers, resist the urge to suggest it would be "better" to share some of the money with her sister. Instead, make the point about sharing by how you talk about what you would do.

After you have done wishes for yourselves, give the game an altruistic spin and talk about wishes for the world. You can talk about how far you think a million dollars would go in feeding all the hungry people in the world. Ask your older children how they would spend their million if they could only spend it on their community.

This is a good way of making your children aware of the problems that others face without making them feel guilty for their own good fortune.

Physical Feats

If your child is squirmy and you are not in the middle of a crowded restaurant, give her some physical challenges to help pass the time. Tell her you are going to organize the "Waiting Olympics" and there are four (or three or five or whatever you decide) events in which she may compete to win. The first is the hop event. She must hop twenty times (adjust the difficulty to fit the age and ability of your child) without letting her other foot touch the ground. The second event is the tiny-step challenge. Your child must cross a distance by putting one foot directly in front of the other so that heel touches toe with each step. The third feat is breath-holding while you recite the alphabet. Keep reciting faster until your child can win. In the final event you name ten different parts of the body, and she moves each one as you name it.

Of course, you can change the challenges to fit the situation and the child. The object is to let your wiggle-worm do a little necessary wiggling.

_____ A WORD ABOUT WHEN _____

This works especially well while waiting in a private examining room for a doctor or in an airport if you can move away into an uncrowded waiting area.

Waiting Out of Line

Have you ever been stuck in a doctor's office or a post office line with a rambunctious or cranky child that couldn't be distracted? Have you had that uncomfortable feeling that strangers around you were thinking, "Problem child; problem parent"? Clearly, those kinds of feelings need to be fended off, but it never occurs to most of us to say to the nurse; "we will be waiting in the hall. Would you come get us there." Or to ask the people in front and back of you to hold your place while you take your child outside for just a minute.

Waiting doesn't have to be in line. People are usually sympathetic to a child's need to squiggle, and often they would rather your child did it somewhere else than on top of their feet. So if the line is long, the wait is weighty and the child is fidgeting, go in the hall or out the door and run a race, play a quick round of Simon Says, order up a few somersaults or whatever it takes to discharge some kid-energy. You, too, will feel much more relaxed letting your child give off steam rather than shushing her for the other adults.

_____ BRASH TRASH _____

It is just one of those days. Your child is in an awful mood and nothing in your repertoire is working. You are beginning to get those looks that you know mean; "Why can't that parent control this child better?" Try this: look at your child with absolute amazement and observe very loudly and very emphatically; "It certainly would seem that this child's parent could figure out how to make her act better!" We promise you will feel better.

Scribble Art

You and your child take turns drawing intersecting lines and curves on a sheet of paper. Then take turns filling in the various areas with different patterns—stripes, solids in different colors, polka dots, plaids, zigzags, and so on.

Doodle Do

Do you doodle while you are on the phone or sitting in meetings? Have you noticed that your doodles usually take on a similar shape? If you are waiting at a table or in an office, try doodling specific shapes with your child. The rule is to keep the pencil from lifting off the page while you doodle a line of triangles. Then do circles and squares. Try curves and S's. See what kinds of patterns you two can doodle from what you have produced.

Alphadesign

Print the letters from A to G here and there on a sheet of paper. Your child connects the letters, going in sequence. As your child learns the sequences of the letters in the alphabet and can recognize them in printed form, add more letters to be connected.

You can do the same thing using numbers. Make it easy at first, then add more; with older children, let them pick out the numbers in the order of a multiplication sequence, like the six table or the eight table.

Shadow Art

When the light is right and you have some paper—like a place mat in a restaurant—and a pencil, you are ready for shadow art. Hold your hand over the paper and talk about the shadow. Let your child trace the shadow on the paper. Then move your fingers—or her fingers—so the shadow is a different shape. Let her trace that and see if you can turn it into something familiar.

UH OH!

This is a good activity to share with a school-aged child. If you are waiting with your family or anywhere where other people are talking, quietly choose a letter that just you and your child know. Whenever you hear a word that begins with that letter, see which one of you can say UH OH first. If others in the family pick up and wonder what you are doing, ask them to guess the letter. It is hard because by the time you say UH OH the conversation has probably moved on several words.

UH OH! TWO

A variation on the theme that works better with younger children is to pick a common word—try "will" or "I"—and try not to use it. If you do, your child tells you, "UH OH." If you get caught five times, you're out. Start over with another word.

3

Bathtime Bubbles

Water is a magic potion. It works a spell on adults and children alike. While we adults may want resorts and lounge chairs and sporting equipment to go with our water, kids are delighted with two cups, three bottles, and one bucket.

It seems a shame that bathtime often comes at the end of the day when kids and parents are tired, because the bath is a wonderful place for fun. The trouble comes when our kids want to have the fun, and we want to bundle them off to bed quickly so we can do the dishes, pay the bills, or just collapse. Allow enough time for bathtime to be a pleasurable activity instead of a necessary evil. Think of the bath not as something to be gotten through but rather as your ten minutes in the day for laughter. If your bathroom is big enough, bring in a chair, but if that's not possible, consider a pillow for kneeling or leaning.

If you have been locked into an end-of-the-day schedule, think about a bath before dinner some nights. Maybe you can have two different kinds of baths. Explain to your child that some nights, when everyone is very busy, you have time only for a Wash Bath. The object of a Wash Bath is to get clean in the least amount of time. You can time yourselves to see how quickly your child can be in, washed, and out, or you can set a sand timer and see if you can finish before the sand is through the hole. But then, on other nights, you should make time for Play Baths. You might have different-colored bath mats that remind your child what kind of bath night it is.

Play Baths can be a pleasurable way for you and your child to end the day. Most children love to play with water and have a wonderful time splashing around in the tub. Keep a rack, a net bag, or a bucket in the bathroom to hold play equipment. Try some of the KIDFUN bathtime games and let your child invent his own. But don't leave young children alone in the bath, even for a few minutes, until you are very sure they are water safe and know the household rules. Never let little children climb in and out of the slippery tub without an older person there.

Working Up a Lather

Using shaving cream or "Crazy Foam" soap, your child can have a great time finger painting the walls of the bathtub. This is a great way to work off steam, and who knows what junior Picassos will be unleashed in the process. It's fun to try with a paintbrush, too.

You might want to save the paintbrush to use as a distraction when washing hair. Children who dislike shampoos can be distracted by scooping up lather from their head for wall painting.

BEAUTY TIP

When washing hair, stop after the first lather and do some hair sculptures. Bring in a hand mirror so your child can admire himself as a work of art.

Tub Aquarium

Cut inexpensive wash clothes or terry kitchen towels of different colors into the shape of fish. Make the fish large enough to be recognized but not so big that they are heavy when wet. At bathtime, direct your child to wash his toes with the red fish and his nose with the green fish. Maybe the yellow fish will be for arms and legs and the green for another place.

CUTTING UP

A fish shape is basically a horizontal oval connected at one end to the point of a squat triangle.

Fizz Whiz

Just for fun, add a little excitement to bathtime with an easy bit of scientific "magic." Break a small piece of an Alka Seltzer tablet and place it in the cartridge from a roll of 35mm film. You can also use a small plastic prescription bottle. Pour water over the tablet to fill the container and put the lid on firmly.

Let your child hold the container and feel the energy gurgling inside. After a minute or so, the solution will erupt, producing a mini-explosion right in the tub. The lid will fly off and the bubbles will trickle down the side of the container. Although the liquid should not be drunk, it isn't harmful, and it won't damage the eyes; but, of course, make sure the container is away from your child's face so he won't be scared or hit.

Magic with Water

Here is more bathroom magic. Have your child fill a plastic cup with bathwater. Then tell him to press a piece of cardboard across the top of the cup. Keeping his hand pressed on the cardboard, he turns the cup upside down. Now he can let go of the cardboard gently sliding his hand away. Magic: The water doesn't spill out. (If you have trouble making this work, use a container with a wider mouth and shorter depth.)

Your child may not understand that the air pressure pushing against the cardboard from below keeps the water from spilling, but he will enjoy the science miracle. You can explain that the same laws of nature that keep the water in help us to keep airplanes flying.

The magic of science is a wonderful catalyst for curiosity. Try another experiment that will fill your child with wonder. Let him crumple up a tissue or paper napkin and stuff it in the bottom of a plastic cup. Have him turn the cup upside down, being sure the paper remains at the bottom of the cup. Then place the cup into the tub of water, being sure not to tilt it. When he takes the cup out of the water, he will be amazed to find that the paper remains dry. (But crumple the paper gently and loosely. If you wad it up too tightly, it will fall out of the cup before the experiment begins.) Later on he will come to understand that the air in the cup pushes against the water, forming an air bubble, and won't permit the water to rush into the cup.

Basketball

For the athletic types, try basketball in the bath. All you need is a small foam ball and a large plastic bowl floating in the tub. Challenge your young person to make three "baskets" in a row or to see how well he can do in six shots. But remind him: NO standing in the tub!

Bath Score

Have a bath with a whole symphony orchestra, the chorus of *My Fair Lady*, Elvis Presley, or Elton John. Bring a battery-operated cassette player into the bathroom and let your child wash to a different score each night. Try classical music to calm a super-wound-up child, rock music when there is time to have some energetic fun, and show music when you want to sing along.

Music at bathtime is especially good when you yourself are feeling wound up and want to calm down.

_____ TOWEL TIP_____

If the cassette or radio is already in the bathroom, jazz up the drying off process by encouraging your little one to dance himself dry by using a big towel and toweling off dance fashion to the beat of the music.

Lullabath

Even if you don't choose to bring marching music or bluegrass into the bathroom, you might try this on days when your cherub is wound extra tight. Bring a cassette recorder with a tape of lullabies into the bathroom and have a very quiet, calm, gentle bath with lullaby music to wind your child down.

SHOWER HOUR

As your child gets older, you may want to help him shift to showers sometimes. A good way to get a child comfortable in the shower is to let girls shower with mom and boys with dad until they are not afraid of getting water on their faces. Once you are comfortable with your child being in the shower alone, you can decide whether morning or night bathing works best for your family.

Scrub-a-Dub-Dub

Have your child gather some cleaning tools that can be used to scrub the tub and tiles above the tub. An old toothbrush, for example, a nail brush, or a scrub brush and a sponge work well. Provide a plastic shampoo bottle that has been thoroughly cleaned. Your toddler will enjoy filling the bottle and squeezing some water onto his brush or sponge.

Your child may decide dolls or toys need a bath too. As he diligently scrubs away at the tub and the walls and the toys, his enthusiasm may spill over to include his own little body in the scrub-down.

Bucket of Buddies

Adults like the solitude of the bath, but children are delighted to have company in the tub. Keep a small bucket in the bathroom filled with different plastic figures. Let you child choose who will get to perch on the tub corners and even go diving for soap on a given evening. You can put words in the play figure's mouth if you like: "Hmmm, did I just hear Big Bird say it was time to soap up and get washed?"

Wash Your Nose; Wash Your Toes

Sometimes it is hard to stop the playing and get your child actually to wash. Try this: Name different parts of the body for your child to wash. Call out the names quickly and choose body parts that are far apart (for example, chin and knee). This makes the game more exciting and cuts down on bathtime by giving the child an incentive to wash quickly. But if you are not in a hurry, add to the fun by using the "Simon Says" feature.

For a variation, sing "Here We Go 'Round the Mulberry Bush." Let your child suggest different parts of the body for each verse as you sing and wash together:

This is the way I wash my hands (legs, toes, nose),
Wash my hands, wash my hands,
This is the way I wash my hands
While I take a bath.

Blowing Bubbles

If you have not already discovered a child's delight in straws, here is your chance. Along with plastic containers filled with fresh water from the faucet, provide some plastic straws. Have your child pour different amounts of water into the containers and then blow bubbles into each container. Is it easier to blow bubbles in a small amount of water or in a large amount?

Challenge her to blow the biggest bathtub bubble in the world, the most bubbles, one hundred tiny, tiny bubbles, or just two bubbles. She will be having fun. You will be running a science experiment.

CAREFUL CAUTION

Very little kids are at risk for breathing in the bubbles. Wait until your children are old enough to help you keep the bubbles away from eyes, nose, and mouth.

Target Practice

After your child has decorated the tub and wall with shaving cream or shampoo, he can have a great time washing it off. Using a water pistol or plastic squeeze bottle, the child aims at the lather target to obliterate the target. Count to see how long it takes.

To test his sharp-shooting ability further, suggest he place light plastic objects, like blocks or small animals, or small paper cups on the inside corners of the tub. The object of the shooting gallery game is to move an object along the ledge of the tub from one corner to another or, if there is no ledge, simply to make the object fall into the water.

Piling several objects on top of each other and letting your child shoot them all down is lots of fun and an excellent way to develop hand-eye coordination.

Sink or Swim

Invite your child to bring some toys into the bath (taking care, of course, to make sure those things cannot be damaged by water). Let him immerse each toy and separate them into the floatables and non-floatables.

If your child enjoyed sorting the floating objects, let him help you search the kitchen for some other things that can go into the tub and be sorted as well. Let him predict what will and what won't float and then check it out himself.

PRACTICAL KNOWLEDGE

You may want to explain about the displacement of mass—how objects that float displace less than their weight in water while objects that sink displace more than their weight. Don't explain too much. This kind of conceptualization will come later. For now your child is storing up *experience*. When his or her brain is developmentally ready for the theory, this youthful experience will help in the learning.

This is true for many children's activities. It is not important at preschool stages that children grasp the concepts but that they have an experiential base on which to pin later learning. If your child asks why, keep your answers simple and straightforward so that "why?" remains a good question, not a prelude to a boring speech.

Shapely Sponges

Get some large, thin sponges at the supermarket. With scissors, cut them into different shapes—maybe a fish or a flower or a football.

Your child can float these unique sponges in the water, and then use them to scrub with instead of a washcloth. You'd be surprised how much more interesting it is to scrub yourself with a yellow football than a plain old washcloth.

A-Sailing We Will Go

No need to buy a fancy fleet of ships for your sailor. Your child will enjoy constructing simple boats of her own to play with at bathtime. Making a raft or a sailboat is easy.

To make the raft, you must first have fun eating popsicles together so you can save the sticks. When you have eaten enough to have twelve sticks, you are ready. Glue eight popsicle sticks side by side. Square off the raft by gluing two more sticks across the rounded ends on each side. Now you have a raft perfect for toy people or animals.

To make a sailboat, have your child cut a triangle out of paper and glue it to a toothpick. Glue or tape the sail stick inside a plastic container or paper cup, and you are ready to set sail.

WORLDLY NOTE

As your children get older they may still enjoy playing with ships in the tub. Stick a plastic laminated map up on the bathroom wall and talk about sailing to Spain or Katmandu or Zanzibar. See if you can get there in only a boat. Use the map to have some fun and teach an early lesson in geography.

In One Pitcher, Out the Other

Children love to fill, empty, and refill containers, pouring back and forth again and again. Give your child a plastic pitcher and plastic containers of various colors and sizes. From time to time, just for a change, add a different size or shape.

Piaget, the famous psychologist who studied child development, realized that children only slowly develop the concept of the conservation of quantity. That is, they will tell you that a tall, narrow pint bowl can hold more than a short, wide pint bowl, even though they have emptied one bowl into the other over and over again. Understanding conservation is developmental and cannot be rushed, but children who have had many experiences pouring and measuring will be ready to embrace the concept as their thinking matures. Besides, they'll have a lot of fun.

Baby's Bath

Put a large rubber doll in the tub with your child. Have him wash the doll part by part, telling you what he is doing as he proceeds. You wash the same parts on him that he washes on the doll.

KID KORNER

Invite some plastic frogs or fish or dolls to a tub tea. Give your child toy cups and saucers and glasses to cater the tub tea.

Bubble Bath

Rushing through our middle years, it is easy to forget how agreeable it is to stretch out in a hot tub frothing with iridescent bubbles and pretend we are having a few minutes in a 1940s movie. Kids are very good for helping us remember this.

Pick a night when you need to relax and your child has done something quite good that day. Reward each of you with a bubble bath. You can do it together or you can dispatch junior and then luxuriate on your own. If you catch yourself thinking, "Hey, I haven't got time for this kind of stuff," repeat after us: "All work and no play does not make for a pleasant earthly stay!" This advice, by the way, works as well for busy dads with aching muscles as for harried moms.

Anatomy Lesson

Everyone can't do this because it requires an under-standing of anatomy, but if you know more about the body than that the knee bone is connected to the leg bone, you might use the bath to have fun teaching your child about parts of the body. One night get him to guess where his solar plexus is. The next, go looking for the esophagus. Ask your child if he is going to wash his vertebrae tonight. Have fun guessing where these funny sounding words might be.

Outhouse Days

On hot summer days, think about outdoor baths. At the end of play time, fill the outdoor pool and let your child soap up with liquid soap, then stand him in the grass and hose him down, roll him up in a big beach towel like a mummy and stretch out on a chaise lounge or in the grass for a few minutes of quiet time.

Or skip the pool and let kids soap up and run in and

out of the hose or sprinkler. You can wash your hair this way, too.

If you live in a really hot climate, think about hooking up an outdoor shower with coils of hose in which the water warms until it's shower time. There is something really wonderful about the smell of summer around you while you shower and then dry off in the sun.

_____ SLIP TIP _____

If you put soap in a kiddie pool, make sure to rinse it out well so the tub is not slippery afterwards.

4

Getting to Bed

Many children resist going to bed even though they are tired and sleepy. Sleep fighters don't want to miss out on anything. But a pleasant bedtime ritual helps children wind down from the day and prepare for sleep. Your child will look forward to spending a bit of happy time receiving your undivided attention; bedtime can also be a warm and satisfying time for you, a time to hear secrets and to lavish affection.

To prepare your child for sleeping, plan a quiet time with her just before you turn out the lights. Try to make this an uninterrupted time. This will help her feel warm and secure in your love. You can hug each other, talk together, sing together, ask real or silly questions, tell old favorite stories, or make up original tales. Encourage your child to join you in expressing her ideas, feelings, and fantasies. Then when you leave her room, her mind can continue to wander in an imaginative world.

For children who have a particularly difficult time saying good-night, one last ritual repeated each night often helps. You might repeat the same rhyme—"When day is done, we stop our fun and say good-night, sweet dreams in sight;" or rub your child's back in the same way each night; or trace the features on her face lightly with your fingers. In this expanded edition, we have added relaxation activities that work especially well for some children.

_____ SEAT TREAT _____

Since bedtime is meant to be a pleasant respite in the day for you, too, make sure you have a really comfortable chair in your child's room. (We like a well-sized rocker that can be pulled up next to the bed.) Having a chair that is really comfortable for parents will make it more enjoyable to talk and read together.

Here are some activities that help children get ready to sleep.

The Magic Carpet

In this KIDFUN activity, you can create a special imagination-filled place for creative storytelling.

Put a bath mat, welcome mat, or small area rug in the middle of the floor and proclaim it the "magic carpet." Sit on this magic carpet with your child.

Have your child close her eyes and imagine she is going to a very special place. Involve her in creative storytelling. Start a tale by saying "Tonight, we are riding our magic carpet to. . . ." Encourage her to fill in the blank. You may need to suggest a place like Disney World, Africa, Mars, or baseball training camp. Let your child build on the story (with you helping as much as needed).

Continue the story for a few minutes, keeping it calm so your child will feel soothed and relaxed. Help her steer the magic carpet to her bed and then roll it up until another night, when you can take a different trip.

A TIP ON TELLING

The best way to encourage creativity is to accept whatever your child says. Enjoy her flow of ideas and images, and be careful not to be judgmental. It is not important that stories make "grown-up sense."

Hum Along

A quiet lullaby is an excellent way to send a child into dreamland. Each week, choose a lullaby to sing each night of that week. You sing it, softly, while your child hums. Then she sings it softly while you hum. And finally, you sing alone and slip from the room humming.

You can use old-fashioned lullabies, contemporary love songs, or folk tunes. Your child may want to suggest songs she has learned in school or day care.

Body Talk

If you sense that your child is especially tense one evening, introduce her to Body Talk. Tell her to lay down in bed, find a comfortable position and shut her eyes. Tell her you want her only to think about what you are saying as you say it. Then begin, in a soft, slow voice to tell her to relax each part of her body: "Relax your toes. Feel your toes getting comfortable and relaxed." Wait a few seconds and then tell her to relax her feet and then her legs and now her hands and arms. Pausing a few seconds between each instruction, continue to tell her to relax her shoulders and neck and head and finally her brain.

Then tell her to feel herself being perfectly relaxed and calm and to think of something happy, something that makes her feel good and peaceful. Now you can run your hand down over her forehead in a relaxing way and tell her that she can relax by letting her body get comfortable and going to this place in her mind anytime she wants.

COPYCAT TIPS

This is not only good for kids but for parents, too. If you have had a crazy-making day and find yourself feeling too tense to enjoy your child, take ten minutes to go into the bedroom by yourself. Take your own body through these relaxation exercises, trying to keep all other thoughts from your mind. Breathe deeply as you relax. Then focus on a time with your child that made you feel very happy and pleased to be parenting. Hold that picture in your mind for a few minutes. See if you don't find some of your own tensions melting.

The Good-night Diary

You may use a school notebook, a pretty bound book, or just a pad of paper for this activity.

Keep a journal with your child that records what was special about that day. Ask your child to think about what was important in her day. Write it down. Some children will have long lists of things they want you to record. Others will need you to ask questions: What made you feel happy today? Did anything make you feel sad or mad today? What did you do today that you would like to do again someday? Tell me something funny that happened to you. Tell me something you learned today that was interesting and that you would like to remember.

If This Day Were an Animal

Turn off the lights and talk with your child about what kind of day she had. Ask her, "If this day were an animal, what kind of animal would today have been?"

This is a wonderful way to teach your children about the animal world. For parents who are interested in animals, reading about different animals and giving your child wider and wider choices can be a great source of fun. A slow summer day might be a turtle of a day, while a mischievous day might be a monkey day, a leaping lizard day, or a foxy day.

Parents can also talk about what kind of day they themselves had. "I had an ant of a day. It just seemed to take me a very long time to get anywhere." Then, "What kind of day did you have?" you might ask your child.

Shapely Descriptions

Create a homemade felt board by gluing a large sheet of felt to cardboard. Make an assortment of shapes for the board by cutting them from different colors of felt. For example, make some big, medium-sized, and small circles, squares, and triangles in blue, red, and yellow. Cut a long strip of black felt, too.

Let your child decorate an envelope, folder, or box to store the pieces. Keep the envelope in the bedroom, and at night you will be ready to play many different descriptive games using the felt board. Take turns giving each other directions by describing objects to put above and below the black strip. One night you might choose to sort the pieces by size, and another by color. Try it this way: Place the black strip across the felt board. Ask you child to find the biggest red triangle and put it above the black line. Then she asks you to find the smallest blue triangle to put above the line. Or, after she finds the largest rectangle, for example, ask her to put the tiniest circle in the middle of the rectangle.

Another night you might organize the pieces by color or shape. Use as many comparison words as you can—words like big, large, huge, gigantic, and less than, bigger than, the same as.

A supply of alphabet letters will add another dimension to this activity. You might buy or make a supply from felt or paper or simply print them all over a large sheet of paper. Have many repeats of the same letter.

Challenge your child to find all the M's, for instance. Time her to see how long it takes. She can pick out the letters (and later count them) or, if you've printed them on a sheet, circle them.

Toy Tales

Many children have a menagerie of stuffed animals in their rooms. Going to bed with a favorite animal or doll can help both boys and girls feel safe and secure. Use a stuffed animal from your child's collection as the leading character in a good-night story. Encourage your child to make up a tale about the animal.

Give her as much or as little help as she needs. You might start the story and then leave out parts for your child to fill in: "Once upon a time there was a lion whose name was. . . . This lion lived in a. . . , and his favorite thing to eat was. . . ."

"And who," you might ask, "do you think, he had for friends?"

Asking leading questions helps to stimulate a child's imagination. Ask, for instance, where the lion most likes to go, who his favorite friends are, and what he thought when he awoke in the morning. Take cues from your child and find the method that works best. Remember: Most children do need help in creating stories.

Reading Together

Every parent knows the value of reading to children. It may be traditional, but it is also wonderful. Studies show that children who are read to are more likely to be readers themselves. Some children want the same book read over and over, while others prefer variety. As your child learns to read, take turns letting her be the reader.

Read your children good books. Consult with the librarian, your child's teacher, or publications that list the best books for children. Find books that are age appropriate but that use language well and stimulate your child's imagination. If you are reading good books, you too will enjoy the reading.

And when your child begins to read herself, don't stop reading to her. Even children who can do "double wheelies" on their two-wheelers find bedtime reading pleasurable. If your children find it hard to let you stop, place a bookmark several pages ahead in the story and stop when you arrive at the mark.

_____ AUTHOR'S CHOICE _____

Our children especially liked *Goodnight Moon*, *A Zoo for Mister Muster*, *Caps for Sale*, and *The Princess and the Dragon*. We liked reading books written by Beatrix Potter, Roald Dahl, and Madelene L'Engle, to name a few.

SuperYou

Of course, reading stories, telling stories and making up stories together is the star bedtime activity for young children. Here is another version of storytelling that let's a child know she is special. Make up a story about a problem solving situation in which your child is the super hero or heroine who saves the day.

For example, your story might twist and turn to reach a line like this: ". . . and so the little lion cub is lost and crying and doesn't know where to go and curls up on the ground, ready to cry—but wait, could it be, is it. . . , yes it's Sally. Sally has come to save the day. Sally knows just what to do. . . ."

My Calendar

If you have a kitchen calendar that tracks family events or a date book you cannot live without, your child might like to have her own personal calendar too. Punch a hole at the top of three-by-five-inch cards and attach them loosely with a metal ring or yarn. On one side of each card write, in sequence, numbers from one to twenty-eight, thirty, or thirty-one, depending on the month.

Each evening, on the reverse side of the card for that day, you or your child can draw a picture of something he did that day. Discuss what happened during the day, and encourage your child to decide what picture he would like to have illustrate that day.

Look ahead in the calendar and write down the important things that are going to happen during the week or the month. You and your child can write reminders to each other on the calendar: "Mom, remember to bring home balloons." "David, make your bed."

Do You Know How I Feel?

Bedtime is the perfect time for close, sensitive talk. Play a game of asking feeling questions that you *both* have to answer. You can ask general questions like these: "How do we feel when something bad happens?" "How do we feel when it seems a friend is being mean?" Or you can ask very specific questions: "What were your feelings when we first saw the doctor today?" "How did you feel when Daddy yelled at Matt at dinner?"

You speak first, and be honest. It will be easier for your child to be honest if you are, and she'll find out that grown-ups have feelings too.

Once you and your child are comfortable with this game, it can help you handle touchy situations and give your child a safe way to get in touch with and talk out her feelings. And it will help you learn about your child.

NOTE OF CAUTION

Never tell a child it is wrong to feel such and such a way or that she doesn't really feel the way she says. If a child says, for example, "I felt mad," and you think she felt scared, you might say, "Sometimes when I first feel mad it is because I am really scared." But don't tell a child, "No, you didn't feel mad, you felt scared," if you want to develop a respectful and trusting relationship.

Picture Friends

If you are going to be away from home for the day, ask your child to look through some old magazines (that you don't mind your child tearing) to find a picture of a child or an animal. Have someone help her cut out the picture and paste it to a sheet of construction paper. At bedtime, talk together about this picture. Ask your child to give the person (or animal) an identity—a name, a family, a friend, a favorite game, a favorite food.

Make a collection of these pictures; your child can choose which one she wants to talk about at night. Perhaps you can introduce one picture character to another. You may find that the pictures serve an educational purpose; instead of lecturing your child on certain behaviors, for example, you can suggest ways the child in the picture would behave.

NOSTALGIA NOTE

Children usually love to hear stories about their parents and siblings. Some evenings you might want to look through some old family pictures together and talk about them.

Flashlight Faces

A neighborhood family first told us about the fun of making ghost faces. Simply cut a mouth, nose, and two eyes from the center of a paper plate. Then, in a dark room, shine a flashlight on the cut-out face and watch the face appear on the wall. Give that face an identity and tell stories about him at bedtime. The next night, try a different face with differently shaped features. Have the two faces meet up with each other and be charmed into a cheerful good-night story. (You may want to avoid scary stories that can create discomfort.)

Shadow Play

This KIDFUN activity is a more active variation on light and shadow, and one that younger and older children can happily play together. Hang or hold a sheet in the center of the darkened bedroom. Shine a flashlight or small light behind the sheet and let one person at a time go behind the sheet and with hands and fingers make shadows on the sheet. Those on the front side can guess what the shadowy figures resemble and make up stories.

This is a super activity for a weekend night when cousins or friends come to spend the night.

Massage

We often make bedtime the time for talking, for reviewing the day, reading stories, trading secrets. Sometimes, however, your child may need touching more than talking.

Gently massaging your child can help her relax and drift toward sleep. What is more relaxing than a back rub? Gently massage your child's back, talking quietly or singing softly. If your child is especially wound up, you might want to start with her feet (except if this is a very tickly child), suggesting she relax and close her eyes. Suggest next she relax her legs and run your finger on the calves of her legs and then her arms. Now suggest she relax her shoulders and lightly massage her shoulders, then her neck, and finally her head. Do this with the lights out and with a very quiet, sing-songy voice, and see if it won't help your child drift toward sleep.

SAFE TOUCHING

Of course, you don't want to touch your child in a sex-
ual way and, as you child becomes old enough to
understand, you can explain that no one should ever
touch your child in a way that makes him or her
uncomfortable or upset. Assure your child that if this
ever happens, you want your child to come and tell
you so you can make sure to fix it. Tell your child that
no matter what, parents are able to help children in
such circumstances when the children ask for help. As
your children get ready for school, explain that people
should only touch our bodies when we tell them it is
okay. "If it does not feel okay with you," tell your child,
"then it is not okay."

Map Rub

This is a special kind of back rub designed to help
your child learn directions and map reading effort-
lessly. Start off scratching or rubbing your child's back
but with directional commentary. As you go up her
back, tell her you are moving north on her back and
then, as you run your finger down it, tell her you are
sailing south. Scratch on the left bone and note that
this is west. Then move to the right—easterly—bone.
Once you have taught your child these directions, let
her tell you where she wants you to scratch or rub by
giving you directions. Some nights, she can be the
scratcher, and you can get your back scratched by giving directions.

Once she has mastered north, south, east and west,
you can add in southeast, northwest, etc. Later you can
reinforce these lessons on a globe or map.

Television Talk

Do you ever wonder how parents managed before television? Most of us have used television as a way to occupy our children when we need time and space for our own activities. But television is also a good vehicle for being together. One night a week, the bedtime activity can be a favorite shared show. Help your child get ready for bed before the program, then snuggle together on the couch, the floor, or a favorite chair watching the program and sharing thoughts.

Because so many of us have video recorders, it is possible to watch the show on our schedule, not the network's. Tape the program you want to watch with your child and put it on when you are ready. Animal and sea world programs are especially good to watch together at night. If you forget to tape, you might rent a National Geographic film, travelogue, or sporting documentary from one of the larger video rental stores.

If television watching is not a usual nighttime activity, this will be a special treat for your child. And if it is, but not usually with you, your child will welcome your involvement. Let someone else in the family take your phone messages and field domestic crises. Treat this like an important meeting and give it your full attention. Your child will get the message that he or she is really important to you.

Tired Twosome

If you have had a hard day and both you and your child are tired, this is for you. Turn out all the lights, lay down beside your child on her bed, assuming she is in a bed big enough to accommodate both of you, and say; "Daddy (or Mommy) is pretty tired tonight, so do you think you could tell me a story while I drift off to sleep. Let's see which one of us can get to sleep first." Then let yourself drift off to sleep right along with your child. If your child is in a small bed, grab a pillow and stretch out on the floor.

HABIT INHIBITOR

You might like this stolen nap so much that you are tempted to make it a habit. This is probably not a good idea because you may find your child only wants to go to sleep when you are lying beside her. Some nights this will not be convenient. Save this for just a few nights when you know nothing else is going to work for you.

Current Events

Your child probably observes members of the family reading newspapers and magazines. Looking through an adult periodical with you will make your child feel quite grown up, especially if there are action pictures and you take the time to talk about them in simple terms. (Although children want to feel a part of parent activities, be careful that in your urge to share your interests and your values you don't slip into a professorial lecture that bores your child. Also, select current event topics wisely.)

Spread the magazine or newspaper picture out between you and help your child notice important details. Help her use her judgment and imagination to draw inferences about what she sees. Some kinds of questions that are good for young children are:

What's happening in this picture?

Do you think these people do this often? Why?

Would you like to do this? How come?

Our four-year-old friend Adam became quite conversant on the last presidential election this way. He recognized the candidates and campaigned for his favorite.

Star Gazers

This doesn't work so well if you live in an apartment building in mid-town Manhattan, but if you are deep into the suburbs, or better, in the country, this is guaranteed to create indelible memories for both you and your child. It may be an annual ritual when your family is on vacation.

When the weatherman tells you there are no clouds, and the temperature is warm enough, let your child stay up until it is dark and then end the day by going outside with sleeping bags or a large quilt to stretch out on the ground and pillows. Lay down together, parents and children, and look at the stars and see what kinds of conversations happen. If you will make time for this to happen, the pleasures will be as much yours as your little ones.

_____ CONVERSATION CLUE _____

Try to avoid questions that need only a yes or no answer.

Tomorrow Talk

Some children like to know what will happen to them on the next day. Talking about what is ahead helps children to develop a sense of planning, goal setting, and the art of logical reasoning for preferential ordering.

Just before that final good-night kiss, you might do a brief review with your child of today and tomorrow. Encourage her to make one realistic plan for tomorrow.

For example, she can decide what to eat for breakfast or she can choose an activity to try while you go to work or plan what window to wave good-bye from. If there is something special on the agenda for the next day—a guest for dinner, a visit to Grandma, shopping for new shoes—this is a good time to mention it. Plan for fun as well as domestic events. This is not a time, however, to urge your child to make a commitment to tasks you want her to accomplish or to introduce stressful events, like a visit to the dentist.

Although a very young child's sense of time is vague, talking about and making plans brings an element of predictability and security into the child's world.

Saying good-night is so warm and satisfying for children that often they don't want to let you out the door. We know a child who always had "Just three more things. . . " to say every time his parent tried to leave.

Instead of leaving abruptly, have a ritual that signals that together time is coming to a close. You might say "Tell me three last things before I go," sing a special exit song, say a series of words together or to each other, or give a special rub of the back or a hug. Once you say it is time to go, stick to your plan. Let your child know that you are serious about bedtime and cannot be wheedled into endless extra innings. If you hold firm, children will usually accept your structure, and saying good-night will be a pleasant experience rather than a struggle for you to get out the door.

Children are more apt to go to bed easily if they know that, once they are put down, they cannot reappear and wander the house. Put a night light on an automatic timer and set the timer so that the light goes on when you think your child should be in bed and goes off at what you consider the acceptable hour for getting up. Explain to your child that when the light is on, she should be in bed—sleeping, thinking quietly, or, if you like, listening to music.

Ghostbusters

Do monsters worry your child? Explain to your worrier that ghosts and monsters live only in people's heads, so we each control our own ghosts and can wish them away. Tell her you can make them go away just with the mind, but sometimes it is good to have extra help. Then give her some specific monster-reduction strategies. You can have a small baggie with magic dust (flour, talcum or powdered sugar all work fine) that you can sprinkle on the edges of the bed to ensure magic dust protection or you can spray them away with a bit of scented monster mist. Try water with some drops of vanilla or mint from a spray bottle.

Face Trace

One of our children especially liked this soothing bedtime activity. At the very end of bedtime conversation, when talk is done and the lights are out, gently trace the features on your child's face—eyebrows, around the outline of the face, down the nose, gently over the lower lip and lightly across the forehead while saying very gently, "Sleep now, sleep well and dream good dreams 'til morning."

5

Cheering Up Sick Days

Often a child is not well enough to go out to play and not sick enough to stay in bed and sleep. The just-sick-enough-to-stay-home child is as likely to feel bad because of boredom as illness. Sitting still all day in front of a television screen leads to restlessness and crankiness; that crankiness can infect the entire family faster than germs.

There are many things a child who is "under the weather" can do to stimulate his mind and imagination. Don't let your child drift into passivity, with little mental stimulation, if he is capable of keeping himself busy and entertained. (On the other hand, if your child is really sick and needs sleep and quiet, let him be.)

A day or two at home, just the two of you, can be a lovely time to work together without interruption on a special project or to build up your emotional relationship. Take advantage of the time to be really together. Talk together, play together, indulge in special treats—cinnamon toast in front of the fire, a popcorn and lemonade tea, milk shakes for lunch. If you cannot give all day to playing, set aside an amount of time when you will stop working and be fully present.

Sick days cannot be planned and are sometimes a real inconvenience for busy parents. But when a little flexibility is possible, they can turn out to be pleasant times for you. If you love to bake but never have time, bring some pillows and blankets into the kitchen and let your child snuggle up while you bake and talk. If you have been avoiding a household project—cleaning closets or scraping paint—put on some music and tackle it while your child works on projects nearby.

Sometimes it is hard to shut out other concerns that are on our minds; our bodies are present but our minds resist. However if circumstances conspire to keep you at home with a sick child on a day when you had plans to be somewhere else, instead of fretting, why not use the time happily, since you are stuck there anyway. You may find that a few happy hours together is good medicine for each of you.

_____ HOT TIP _____

If your child needs to work in bed, give him a large tray or the top of a large cardboard box to work on. Place an old towel or sheet on the bed to protect it.

Alphabet Fun

Give your child some sheets of paper (colored paper works well), paste, and a box of alphabet cereal. He is ready to create designs, words, or letter searches randomly by pasting cereal on the paper. Then suggest he look for all the letters in his name or all the letters that have a circle in them.

Babies Book

Gather up a collection of family baby pictures. Include your child and his siblings, but also look for pictures of parents and grandparents, aunts, uncles, and cousins. Your child will have fun trying to identify family members and comparing their looks then to their appearance now. Children love to hear stories about themselves as babies and about the childhoods of other family members.

―――――――――― EXTRA CREDIT ――――――――――

This is a wonderful activity for a child to do with a grandparent.

Mirror Mirror

Even the littlest child is fascinated by mirrors. A non-breakable mirror is a good addition to a crib or playpen.

A child who is a little older and has learned to draw might like to use a mirror to do self portraits. One might be just with pencil and paper, another with crayons. The point, of course, is not portrait quality art but the fun of looking and reflecting on oneself.

Puppet Theater

A pleasurable quiet activity for the child who should keep still is puppet or stuffed-animal theater. Ask your child to create a little entertainment for you over lunch (dinner, snack). Pick a few characters. Some children will have no trouble starting off on a story line. Others will welcome a few organizing hints. Either way, ask your child to make up a play, rehearse it, and present it to you. If you have the time, take a puppet of your own and create a story together. Perhaps you will decide to put on the puppet play for the rest of the family at dinner.

Crazy Zoo

This project involves a little art, a little storytelling, a dollop of imagination, and a lot of fun. Your child closes his eyes and scribbles on a sheet of drawing paper. When he opens his eyes, he examines the scribble and decides how he can make it into a crazy animal. For example, he can add ten eyes, three ears, four tails, and one top hat—anything at all.

Encourage him to make many crazy animals and to give them crazy names. Our friend Jason had an oplop and an eelatormay and a shiny, shooting spark doork in his zoo one rare day. Like Jason, your child can arrange his animals into a crazy zoo and entertain the family with stories about the members of his zoo.

A Stitch in Time

Many children, boys as well as girls, enjoy sewing. One way to help your child practice some small motor skills is to cut out two identical patterns in the shape of clothing—a shirt or pants or a dress. Holding both pieces together, use a hole punch to punch holes around the edges and—with a string, rope, shoelace, or a piece of yarn in a large children's embroidery needle—let your child stitch the pieces together.

Older children can practice sewing skills by sewing buttons on a piece of cloth or making a small quilt from scraps.

_____ TIP-END TIP _____

If a needle isn't handy, try wrapping a small piece of
cellophane tape around the edge of the yarn to create
a sharp point.

Fashion Designer

Make a small, simple person shape from heavy cardboard. Glue on a face that fits. It can be the face of a
model from a fashion magazine, a picture of your
child's face or someone from an advertisement. Then,
also from cardboard, cut patterns for clothes: a shirt,
pants, a dress, a skirt. Using recycled gift paper, colored paper and bits of whatever arts and craftsy stuff
you have around, your child can trace the pattern onto
paper and design a jazzy wardrobe for this cutout doll.

_____ STOCK UP _____

Invest in some yarns, a large hook-in needle (instead of
one with an eye to thread), and sheets of plastic grid.
These can be bought in already organized boxes or
piecemeal. Let your child make a wall hanging, a belt,
or whatever else her imagination suggests.

Color Memory

Gather a group of small objects, each with a distinctive color and shape: for instance, a yellow feather, a
red heart, a black checker, a brown crayon. Let your
child examine them carefully. Then, place them in a
box and blindfold your child. He puts his hands in the

box and, one by one, removes each object, feeling it and remembering what color it is. Remove the blindfold and let him see how well his memory is developing.

Table Decorations

As children get older, they like a sense of purpose in their activities. Suggest to your sick child that you and he surprise the family with table decorations for dinner that evening. Let him design placemats, name cards, and room decorations, and decorate the eating area for dinner. If there is time and energy, you may want to make a special dessert as well.

Fishy Art

Put your child to work looking for pictures of fish in books, magazines, and the encyclopedia, studying their distinctive features—fins, tails, gills, and special designs.

Then have him design an aquarium with fish of his own. It is easy for children to draw a fish by making a circle or oval and adding a triangle to one end. After coloring the fish with various stripes and spots, have him cut them out and mount them against one or more large sheets of blue construction paper (in a pinch, substitute silver foil). Add seaweed by cutting strips of green paper in a curvy pattern and pasting them here and there. With chalk, your child can add some bubbles and waves. When all is in place, put a sheet of clear plastic food wrap over the top to give the scene a shimmery, watery effect.

An alternative is to make a fish mobile by attaching the fish to the ends of different lengths of string and tying them to a hanger.

_____ FEELING AMBITIOUS _____

You can make this project more complex by cutting out two large fish of the same shape, one just a little bigger than the other. Have your child color both shapes (on appropriate sides), then staple them halfway together. Stuff crumpled tissue paper, paper toweling, or newspaper between the pieces and finish stapling for a two-dimensional fish mobile.

Geometric Wares

Have your child cut many circles, rectangles, and triangles of different sizes out of construction paper. Now he can combine them in different ways to create all kinds of objects for a pretend story. For example, he can make a long train by pasting circles (for wheels) under rectangles (for cars) and linking them with small black strips. He can create robots and sailboats and ice-cream cones and any other thing his imagination envisions.

Sneak a Peek

Start by having your child cut out pictures of animals or other objects from magazines. After she has pasted pictures on several pieces of paper, challenge her to a guessing game. Using the same size paper your child used, cut a smallish hole in the sheet of

paper. Choose one picture and cover it with your sheet
of paper. See if she can identify the object just from
what she sees through the hole.

You may want to make two—or three—small holes
in different parts of the paper, or you may want to
move the paper around a bit if more clues are needed.

Creative Jewelry

Making jewelry—necklaces, bracelets, and pins—is
a particularly absorbing activity for many children
and can be adopted to various ages. Younger children
can string together popcorn, rigatoni noodles, or Cheerios with a large needle and thread to create original
jewelry. Small marshmallows, squares of colored
paper, and buttons can be used in lieu of semiprecious
stones. After the stringing, your child can paint each
bracelet or necklace the favorite color of each person in
the family. For older children, a supply of inexpensive
beads can be absorbing.

To make pins, cut out circles or abstract shapes from
heavy cardboard for the backing and let your child
fashion pins by gluing on beans, scraps of cloth, and
other odds and ends. Add a strong safety pin to the
back or punch a hole in the top, thread with yarn, and
wear as a necklace.

Handy Helper

Children like to feel helpful, and a sick day may be a
good time to put your child to work at a real activity.
Have him stack the pennies in the penny jar in piles of
ten for rolling, sort the socks by matching colors, line

up the cans in the pantry in a neat arrangement with all the labels facing front, or dust the books on his bookshelf. Perhaps this is a good day to organize the toys and to hunt for missing pieces.

Storytelling

Sick days are wonderful days for reading aloud; one parent we know keeps one really good reading in reserve for just such a long day. If you are in a time crunch and are not able to read but want your child to rest quietly, think about a cassette tape with a story. These can be bought, borrowed from the library, or made at home. If your child is not too sick to go out briefly, an early-in-the-day trip to the library may give you just what you need for a perfect day together.

GUILT SAVER

If you must be at work while your child is ill, tape a story the night before. Leave it for your child to listen to during the day. At the end of the story, leave him a personal message and ask him to tape you an alternative end to the story for you to listen to with him when you get home.

Movie Time

For a child who has discomfort—perhaps she is itching with the chicken pox or cranky with a sore throat—renting a movie may be just the ticket for distraction. With younger children, you must, of course, watch at their level. With older kids, you can have the fun of introducing your child to some of your old favorites that no one else in the family wants to watch.

<hr>

MOVIE GUIDE

Try the standards like "Wizard of Oz", "Fantasia", "101 Dalmatians" or "E.T." See how the old Charlie Chaplin and Laurel and Hardy silent films are received, and ask friends what has entranced their children.

Room Signs

If you can manage to lay your hands on two sheets of rub off letter and/or letter tracer sheets, (look in an office supply store or, sometimes, the stationery aisle of your local pharmacy) you can offer your child a quiet activity that can be done in bed or tucked in a corner near you while you are working.

Get your child started making signs for around the house. The first might announce that your child is sick: "JASON IS SICK." He can rub the correct letters, "MOM AND DAD'S ROOM," or "JASON'S ROOM" on a big sheet of paper and decorate around them. You might get him to make reminder signs: "DID YOU BRUSH?"and "DID YOU FLUSH?" for the bathroom and "SMILE" for the mirror.

Even a child who is not yet much of a speller can hunt for the letters if you write out the words. Very little children might like to make their own free-hand door signs for the day.

Button Box

Do you drop buttons into a box or a jar when they come attached to new clothes or fall off old ones? Organizing your buttons is a good stuck-in-bed activity. Gather up the buttons and let your child sort them out for you, using margarine dishes or baggies. All the small white ones can go in one pile. All the large white ones in another. All the dark ones in still another and then the fancy colored ones for the last pile. This is an easy, quiet diversion that can be done on a bed tray, but, of course, it is only for children old enough to know not to put the buttons in their mouths or other orifices.

Stringy Stories

Children with a fever may be most content leaning against you while you read or listen to tapes together. A child who is a little less sick might like to help you make up a story. Take a long piece of string or rope and sit down on the floor together. Place the string in a circle and ask your child what it reminds them of. Make that the starting point for the story. At various points, one or the other of you should reshape the string, using the shape to imagine something else, and so the story progresses.

For example, if your child looks at the circle and says "a sun," then you begin the story on a bright sunny day but if she says "pie," you take off in a different direction. From time to time, stop the story and look at the string for inspiration. Make it a wiggly line, a straight line, a bigger and smaller circle and so on.

Both you and your child will be exercising imagination and the odds are you will get silly with this string and find yourselves laughing, too.

Match the Batch

Grab two paper bags—brown lunch bags are good—and find a collection of tactile objects around the house, making sure you have two of each. Try cotton balls, silk squares, feathers, wool, different shaped buttons and sponges cut into small pieces, for example. Now your child is ready to be the Fine Fingered Magician!

Without looking in the bag, have your child select one object from the first bag and then find its mate in the second bag. Count how long it takes each time.

Footprints

Your "little energy machine" has definitely got a run-down battery and may not be found in any of his usual places when the family comes home at the end of their day. Suggest he create a trail that will allow family members to come immediately to the bedroom—or wherever he is cuddled until fully recharged.

Have him stand with each foot on a piece of plain white paper. Trace around each foot, including the space between the toes. Then cut several copies of each foot. Encourage your child to design the most imaginative feet he can—purple feet with green and pink polka dots, feet with stars and feet with bright yellow toenails. When he has designed as many feet as his attention span permits, place the feet around the house, starting at the front door and leading directly to where your child is.

Clean Machine

Okay, you are stuck at home with a sick child and it wasn't what you planned. You have a desk full of work at the office or a to-do list to choke a horse. You can try to keep to your schedule and, perhaps, come up very frustrated at the end of the day, or you can do the absolute minimum and bag the rest. See the day as an opportunity. Make it a time out for you as well as your child. Think about what you have been wanting to do at home.

Dig up all your old records or tapes from your past and listen to them while you reorganize the kitchen, the basement, or whatever else you have been meaning to do that never seems to get to the top of the list. Make your child a part of this by piling quilts and pillows on the floor nearby. If he is well enough, give him small, age appropriate jobs. Remember that the goal is not to get the job done in record time but have a nice time while getting something useful done.

As the old songs remind you of stories about your past, share them with your child. Ask him to decide which one is his favorite.

Magazine Reading

You and your child can spend many happy hours poring over magazines. There is wonderful, stimulating material here for the nonreader.

For example, use pictures for categorizing activities: Search for and cut out all the beverages or tall buildings or boats. Look for all the pictures with red or all the pictures where people are smiling. If someone in your family has a particular interest, make a booklet for that person. Cut out all the fashion jeans advertisements for an older sister or all the sports pictures for Dad.

You can do wonderful picture interpretation, encouraging your child to use his eyes and mind to scrutinize pictures—drawing inferences (Why are they carrying suitcases?); discovering spatial (Which is closer to us, the house or the horse?) and interpersonal (Why is the man holding the child?) relationships; exercising judgment (Would this animal make a good pet?); and drawing conclusions (How do you think the window got broken?).

The next ten activities suggest some other specific ways that you can plumb the magazine gold mine.

COLLECTOR'S CORNER

If you do not subscribe to a number of picture magazines, keep the magazine sections from the Sunday newspaper and some of the sections and advertisements with pictures. Pile them up in a storage area for a day when you will need them.

Magazine Collages

APPETIZING MENUS

Give your child a supply of paper plates and ask her to prepare some delicious meals. The "cooking" is done by looking through magazines for pictures of food, cutting them out, and pasting them on the plates. Afterward, dolls and stuffed animals can be invited to breakfast, lunch, dinner, or a holiday party.

INITIAL POSTER

Write the initial letter of your child's first name at the top of a sheet of paper. Encourage your child to look through a newspaper or magazine for a picture of objects—or words themselves—that begin with the same letter. Cut them out and paste them on the poster. Afterward, print the word under each picture.

SEASONAL WORK

Make a picture book of the seasons by cutting out pictures of the various seasons and grouping them accordingly. Your child can add his own drawings of things he likes to do in each season.

LIKE LETTERS

Print a different letter of the alphabet at the top of several pages of a magazine. Your child scans the page to find words that begin with the letter you have written at the top. He circles each word he finds. Later, you can help him count the words for each letter and decide which was the most popular.

MY FAVORITES

Spend some time talking about favorite things: favorite foods, favorite toys, favorite cars, favorite clothes. Let your child look through the magazines for pictures of favorite things to cut out and paste on pages to make a book.

FAMILY FAVORITES

If you have grandparents or favorite relatives in other cities, let your child dictate a cover note and mail off the favorites book to some favorite person.

I'VE GOT YOUR NUMBER

Give your child a book or magazine and ask her to find a specific page number. Time her as she does this. Then give her another page number to find. Keep a score card so she can see which numbers she found easily and which were more troublesome. If you save the score cards over a period of time, you can compare them, see how much progress she is making, and identify the numbers that seem more difficult.

NAME COLLAGE

Use the newspaper headlines for this. Put your child to work cutting out letters that are in his name, getting many different samples of each letter. He then can arrange the letters to spell his name in many different styles. With paste, let him arrange his name collection in a collage on the paper.

AND SO ON

Beginning readers may enjoy hunting the page for a particular word. Write a common word like "the" or "on" or "and" at the top of the page. Your child can then circle or underline the word every time he finds it. Afterward, he can count how many times the word appears.

SETTING UP

Write a number from one to five on the top of five blank sheets. Give these to your child. His job is to search through magazine and newspaper pages to find items in the same category. The page with a 1 needs only one item, but the page with a 2 needs two pictures of the same object—two shoes or two refrigerators or two babies—and so on.

MY MAGAZINE

After exploring your collection of magazines, your child may be ready to produce his own. Give him some sheets of paper, paste, and crayons and tell him to make his own magazine about anything he wants. When he is finished, have him "read" his magazine to you.

6

Rainy Days Need TV Alternatives

R ain, rain go away. Come again some other day.
One rainy day can seem as long as Noah's forty in the ark when an active, out-of-doors child finds herself unwillingly confined inside. Dreary rain or icy weather may dampen our own spirits as well, making it harder to cope with cranky or restless moods that bad weather can trigger in our children.

Avoid the rainy day blahs by keeping your child active, mentally and physically, with simple games, art projects, and creative dramatics such as those described here. Invite a friend to join your child if that is possible, but know that there are many things here a child can happily do with you or alone that will provide far more learning and pleasure than spending the day glued to the television set.

Watch, too, for a break in the bad weather, and consider a few minutes outside for a fresh-air break on a bad day. When the sun comes out after the rain, you might think of going on a "rainbow alert."

And even if it is not rainy, you will find good ideas here for all kinds of children in all kinds of weather.

Wet Chalk

A wet day is a day for wet chalk. In the morning, soak some colored chalk in a solution of three parts water to one part sugar for two or three hours. (The sugar reduces the dusty quality of the chalk when it eventually dries up.)

Then let your child draw on construction paper—black is best—or a home blackboard and have fun with the lovely deep colors and textures this medium produces.

Dress-up

A rainy day is a great day for dress-up. Think about keeping a box or bag of old clothes just for dress-up. Let your child try tottering in high heels (even little boys think this is great fun) or clumping in Daddy's biggest shoes, stuffed with socks in the toes; vamping in long shawls, prancing around in cowboy hats; and dancing with a cape made from an old skirt, sheet, or towel. Little girls love messing with Mommy's jewelry and having their nails painted red and their faces painted with a star or a smile.

Give your child some character parts and have her come back costumed and ready to act for you. You might suggest she dress as Superman with a cape, a cowboy with a bandana and boots, an old woman with a cane, or a visitor from another planet with a helmet. She can then act a part and let you guess the character.

COSTUME SHOP

Wonderful presents can be found at theater prop shops and costume stores. A cardboard top hat, a walking stick, or inexpensive white gloves can transform an ordinary kid into a dazzling dancer. A clown nose, big feet, a plastic bow tie, or a wig will be a cherished gift, bringing hours of pleasure and gallons of giggles.

Balancing the Books

Suggest that you and your child invent a new Olympic event: book balancing. Challenge her to walk around the room balancing a storybook on her head without letting it fall off. She must not touch it with her hands at any time. She will quickly discover the importance of walking very carefully with her head held high. Let her try books of different sizes and shapes to decide which one is the easiest and which the hardest to balance.

This activity can become a contest, with everyone in the group participating. One person acts as the judge while the others try to balance books on their heads. Everyone walks around the room at the same time, and the winner is the one who keeps the book on the longest without touching it. This person then becomes the next judge, who asks contestants to change the size and weight of the books for another round of balancing.

Color Day

When your child wakes up one morning and complains that it is raining and there will be nothing to do, introduce her to "Color Day."

Ask her to pick one color to focus on for the whole day. Suppose the color is red. Have her pick out clothes with red in them. Look for breakfast, lunch, and dinner foods that are red and make red decorations for the table. Red art projects, red painting, and word hunting for the word "red" can be activities during the day. Hunt through magazines for pictures with red. Count all the things in your house that are red. Let your daughter help think up new "Color Day" activities as the day progresses.

The Hand Is Quicker Than the Eye

Place three identical paper cups upside down in a horizontal row on the table. While your child watches you carefully, place some small object—a button, a checker, or a stone—under one of the cups. Tell your child to keep his eyes glued to the cup as you rearrange the cups by sliding them along the table several times in different configurations. Challenge your careful observer to point to the one roaming cup that hides the object.

Your child will love taking turns with you and trying to trap you. You might chant a little abracadabra song:

Watch my hands with your eyes.
But don't be taken by surprise,
As these cups go sliding by.
There's only one you have to spy.

ALL-GENERATION ALERT

This activity is a hit with all ages. Try it during grand-parents' visits too.

Musical Interlude

Strike up the band with musical instruments you've created out of ordinary materials you have in your home. For example, to make your own maracas, you will need the cardboard cylinder from inside a toilet paper roll; aluminum foil; dry beans (or buttons); and two rubber bands. Help your child cut two circles or squares (about four inches across) from the foil. She covers one end of the toilet paper roll with a piece of foil and puts a rubber band around the foil to close off the end securely. Then turn the roll over, carefully drop some beans inside the roll, and cover the other end in the same way. Now she has a maraca for shaking and dancing to.

Collected pebbles, buttons, or marbles inside a metal salt shaker or tin tea canister are also good for shaking.

When the tinny sound gets to you, set your child to looking for bits of wood or wooden objects around the house (for example, a wooden spoon, a small cheese board, wooden molds, clothes pins). Striking or scraping two of these wooden objects together slowly or quickly, hard or soft, will add some interesting beats to her dance music.

She can have a rhythm band by putting on a record or tape and using her homemade instruments to play and sing along with. If the noise level exceeds your tolerance, challenge your musician to see how softly she can play her instruments.

Pick Up Sticks

This traditional game can be enjoyed even by little children. Use ten popsicle sticks, plastic swizzle sticks, or plastic straws. Your child holds the sticks together in one hand, then lets them go, dropping the sticks on the table. She tries to pick them up, one at a time, but she must be very careful not to make another stick move while picking one up. If she moves one, her turn is over for that round. Count how many sticks she retrieves each turn or how many turns it takes her to pick up all the sticks. See if she can improve her score with practice. You try it next.

Musical Animals

Have some fun introducing your child to the high and low notes on the piano. Hit a deep note repeatedly in a deliberate slow rhythm. Encourage your child to listen carefully and then walk like an animal the music reminds her of—perhaps an elephant, a hippo, or a bear.

Then switch to a high note and play it in a faster beat, suggestive of a different kind of action. Your child should change her pace accordingly, perhaps imitating the movements of birds, mice, cats, or monkeys.

Give your child a chance to strike the piano keys and to experiment with notes and what they suggest.

If you don't have a piano, you can use a toy drum to beat slow, deep sounds or quick, light beats. Look around the house for other objects you and she can use as instruments—such as a large plastic container and two wooden spoons—and experiment with the sounds.

Treasure Hunt

Children love the excitement of hiding and searching, so play hide-and-seek or have a treasure hunt with toys or household objects. When you are ready for a change, add a learning component to this activity.

Choose one letter of the alphabet for a child just learning to recognize letters. Send her from the room while you hide several pieces of paper with the letter written on it. (Don't hide the papers too well, or your child will become frustrated.) Now call your child back and announce, "I have hidden six T's in hiding places in the room. See how fast you can find them." If she has difficulty, call out "hot" or "cold" to give her clues as she moves closer to or farther from the hiding spots.

For an older child, write the letters of her name or a new word on paper and cut them out like a puzzle. After the pieces are found, make fitting the pieces together (with your help if necessary) part of the game.

Still older children can go on a scavenger hunt in the house, looking for six objects that have two vowels in them (like sheet, towel, soap, chair, book, paper), ten objects that start with T, or a list of specific things you have made up. Make returning all the objects within a certain amount of time another game, afterward.

Dental Care

A rainy day is a good day to make sure the dolls and stuffed animals in your house are getting good dental care. Have your child make a toothbrush. Start with a popsicle stick, which your child can color with crayon. Then have her cut out a small rectangle of paper, about one third the length of the stick and four times the width. Fold the paper in half and make zigzag cuts in the two edges. Then slide the stick between the two sides of the paper and paste the zigzag edges together. Now she can go to work on her victims' teeth. If she insists on toothpaste, try a little talcum powder (but remind her that talcum is not for people's teeth).

Indoor Volleyball

Need a little indoor exercise? Balloons are the answer. They are small and light and 92 percent damage proof.

Let your child have fun just bouncing the balloons in the air with one hand, or two at a time, or in alternating order. Or organize a volleyball game by tying a string between the tops of two chairs that are placed some distance apart. Two or more children can have fun hitting the balloon back and forth.

BALLOON BONUS

Keep a bag of balloons handy. They are good for all sorts of diversions: a game of catch, mock badminton with magazines for paddles, rolling races where the object is to blow the balloon across the room. They can cheer up a sick room, or festoon the dinner table along with a recipe created with your child's fertile imagination.

What's Missing?

Place five objects on a tray—a key, a ball, a spoon, a block, and a crayon, perhaps. Have your child look carefully at all the objects and name each one she sees.

Then have her close her eyes while you remove one object and put it in your pocket. She reexamines the tray and decides what is missing. Gradually add more objects to the tray, and when she gets really proficient, remove more than one object to make the game especially challenging. The whole family can enjoy taking turns playing this game.

A variation is to blindfold a guesser and have her feel all the objects on the tray and determine which one is missing by her sense of touch.

To prolong the game, hide the object you remove in the room and play "hot and cold" (calling out "hot" when she's near the object, and "cold" when she's far away) while your child hunts for the missing object.

I Know What I Feel

Blindfold your child with a scarf or a dish towel. Instruct her to walk carefully around in the room with her arms outstretched. She moves around until she touches some object, which she must describe and identify. Then it is your turn to be blindfolded and touch and tell. Compare notes with your child to see which she thinks is more fun—to be doing the groping or to watch you doing it.

Of course, make sure you are in a room that is free of dangerous obstructions or precious Chinese vases. And make sure you are there, standing by, while the blindfold is on.

Escape

On days when you can't go out, it is terrific fun for children to go in—into caves made from large cardboard boxes, the larger the better, and tents made from draping blankets or sheets over a table. You provide the setting, and your child's imagination is likely to provide the theatrics.

Younger children can color or paint their boxes. Older children can work with scissors to cut windows and peep hatches in the boxes.

The Bridge to Adventure

Organize an obstacle course that leads to high adventure. Set up a bridge with a bench, two chairs side by side, or just a rope on the floor that must be walked on. Beyond this bridge, set up obstacles with your child that he can jump on, hop around, or crawl under, over, into, onto, or behind. A sofa can be crawled behind. A wooden chair can be crawled under. A stool can be stepped on. A bag of laundry can be jumped on, and a plastic laundry basket can be sat in. Cartons, step stools, and large baskets can be made into other obstacles.

Now add some imagination. Tell your child that the bridge leads to an exciting, imaginary world. Help him create a story about some place he would like to go and something he would like to do there. He can enter this world by crossing the bridge, visit all the sights, and return to the bridge to start on a new journey again and again. He may go to an amusement park and ride a rocket (stand on the stool) or swim in a lake (lie on a blanket with motion). He may take off to the Galaxy or Dorothy's Oz or Mickey Mouse's Disneyland. He can explore a haunted house, go to the circus, and romp with Peter Pan all on a rainy afternoon.

This is a wonderful game to play with friends. Don't be surprised if setting up the course is half the fun and takes much longer than the journey itself.

Animal Charades

Ask your child to think of an animal but not tell you which one. You try to guess as she imitates the animal as best she can. Her job is to help you guess as quickly as possible.

Once you guess, you take a turn. After each of you has guessed successfully, talk about animals with your child. List all the different animals she can name. Try to find pictures of some of them. Sort the animals into three groups: wild animals, farm animals, and pets. Find out more about the animals you acted out earlier.

See if you can be better imitators with what you have learned. Plan a trip to the zoo some sunny day soon.

As with so many of these activities, your discussion with your child will enrich her vocabulary and her understanding of the world.

—————— ANIMAL WATCH ——————

If your child is especially engaged by this KIDFUN activity, rent animal movies from your local video store and enjoy learning together.

A Book of Cats

If your child is interested in animals, this will entertain her. Look through books and magazines together to find pictures of different animals in the cat family. Talk about the differences in cats. Then encourage your child to make her own cat book. She can draw cats, trace cats, or cut out pictures of cats. Make one page for each cat. She can glue yarn or paper to her pictures to give the cats stripes and spots, and she can design her own breed of cat. She might like to name each cat.

Collect all the pictures, and staple or string them together and create a book. Put a title on the cover and have your child sign it as the author.

Homemade Hopscotch

If you have a busy body that insists on lots of exercise, here is a way to satisfy those large motor needs indoors. Try taping a hopscotch board to the floor with tape. Do this in an unfinished basement, an attached garage, a covered porch, or an open space in the kitchen. Chalk can be an alternative in the garage.

You may remember that you start playing hopscotch by tossing a small pebble onto the drawn squares, making sure it lands inside the first square and does not touch any lines. You repeat this in numeric order. That is, you first toss the pebble into square one, then two, and so on. Once the pebble is in the right square, you must hop on one foot through the squares in numerical order, pick up the pebble, turn around at the end, and return, without losing your balance or stepping on a line. (You can land on two feet when the squares are side by side and when you are turning around in the end zone.) You keep hopping until you step on a line or lose your balance; then the other person takes over. The first person to complete the process, from one through eight, wins.

For a simpler challenge and/or a smaller space, make a number line by placing two five-foot strips of masking tape on the floor a foot apart. Divide this into one-foot squares by taping across the space between the two tapes at one-foot intervals. Write the numbers one to five in the boxes with tape.

Now call out a number from zero to five. Your child must hop onto that number and jump that many times. (You can count together.)

If you want to work on number recognition with your child, hold up a card that has a number on it from zero to five. As before, your child hops onto that number and jumps that many times, counting as she jumps. Or your child chooses the number secretly, hops there, and tells you what it is. Ask her to move ahead or back one or two boxes, or give her easy math problems: "Three plus two, how many is that?" "Four minus three, how many is that?"

Sign Language

Introduce your child to the concept of sign language. Talk about hearing and about other ways of understanding people. Make up some signs that can be a special language in your family. If your child is interested in sign language, go to the library together and find a book on American Sign Language. Learn some of the simple signs together. Try "I love you," "good night," "sweet dreams" and "What's for dinner?"

Rough Work

Recently, we have come to understand more about how people learn. Each of us has different gifts, and we learn best when we can use our natural gifts and aptitudes. Verbal learners like to hear things. Visual learners like to see things. Many children do best when they can feel and manipulate materials. Here is a project that will help all young children learn numbers and letters, but will be especially good for children who learn best by touching.

You will need a few sheets of sandpaper. If you are buying sandpaper, get an assortment of grades so that you'll have different textures and surfaces.

If you have cardboard or wooden letters and numbers, your child can trace around these on the sandpaper. If not, you can write on the sandpaper with a magic marker (keep the letters and numbers small enough to fit on a note card). Cut them out and paste each one on a three-by-five-inch card. These cards are excellent learning tools. Have your child close her eyes and feel a card, using her fingers to discover the letter or number. The tactile impressions will reinforce visual learning.

Some other rainy day, you can convert these cards into an alphabet or number book by having your child draw or cut and paste a picture on each card that begins with the letter or matches the number.

Car Race

If match box cars or other small-wheeled vehicles are popular in your house, organize races against the clock. Set up a long track with tape or string on the floor. Make sure there is a start and a finish line. Using a kitchen timer or a stopwatch, let your children organize car races along the track and see who gets the best time.

HOUSEKEEPING HINT

If the cars are in danger of veering into a wall or furniture, use bolsters or pillows for protection.

Connect the Raindrops

If it isn't raining too hard, open the window and let your child hold a piece of construction paper or gray cardboard out the window. Tell her she must pull it back in by the time you count to five. When she pulls it back in, you'll see dark spots from the water. Let your child connect the dots quickly with pencil or crayon in any sequence she wishes. After they dry, she can experiment with filling in sections of her rain design.

Library Hunt

In this high-tech age of e-mail and computer games, it is still important to be on familiar terms with the printed page. So on a rainy day put on your duck boots, head for the library, and hunt up something interesting.

Before you go, get your child to help decide what kind of book you will look for—something with dinosaurs or one with a little boy and his grandpa or a book that is sure to have trains or planes?

As your child gets older, help her to learn how to use the newer computerized card catalogues. If you don't know, you can learn together. Look to see how many authors share your last name and what they write about. Pick a subject and figure out how and where the books are organized. Find out what team won the baseball pennant the year your child was born or the recipe for chocolate chip cake and see how long it takes you in your search.

Imprints

This is a project that lots of parents find absorbing themselves. Organize some drawing paper and paints—tempera, poster, or watercolor paints will all work.

Have your child round up some small objects with different shapes and textures: a piece of sponge, a bottle cap, a seashell, a margarine top, and some pencil erasers are good starters. Now let her dip the object into the paint and use the wet object as a stamp to print designs on the paper. She can experiment with repetitions and with different shapes on one page.

After she has experimented with these objects, try

some new ones. A citrus fruit cut in half and dipped in paint makes a beautiful effect on paper. Cutting a potato in half, and gashing holes and gullies in it will also produce interesting designs. Improvise with what you have on hand and see what else makes good imprints.

_____ USEFUL RESULT _____

When your daughter gets the technique perfected, let her make imprints on plain paper or folded notes to use either as thank-you notes from her or as gifts to others in the family.

Aerospace

Kids are fascinated by rockets and planes. Build on that interest by looking in magazines or books at pictures of rockets. Observe the basic structure of the ship—its shape, the flame underneath, the capsule on top. Point out that the basic shape is a rectangle with a triangle on top.

Invite your child to design some rockets, color them, and cut them out. Now she can make a rocket mobile by gluing different-length strings to each (or punching a hole in each and threading the string through it) and attaching all the rockets to a hanger. You can display the rockets from the ceiling, in a doorway, or in a window.

Computerizing

Many households now have computers, and kids are never too young to be introduced to this marvelous machine. Sit with young children and have them type single letters on the keyboard—repeating a row of A's then B's, for example. Print a few simple words in large print and help your child find the letters on the keyboard and copy the words. Try typing her name in a variety of ways: caps, bold, underlined, in different fonts.

Spend some time browsing in a computer store with educational software to see if you can find computer programs that will be fun and educational for your child. Very young children may not yet have adequate coordination for computer games—but they learn very quickly if there are older children around to demonstrate. For older children, buy a typing program—there are several that teach touch typing but make the learning process fun—and encourage your child to spend some regularly scheduled time each day beating her score and learning the keyboard. (It works for adults, too!)

One Fisted Lottery

This simple "board" game can be played with children of all ages and with nothing more complicated than a piece of paper a pencil and some stones or pennies.

You know the game of putting both hands behind your back, clenching an object in one and then putting your hands out for someone to guess which one holds the object? Well, this is an old Indian game built around this guessing idea but with a way of tracking how good a guesser you are.

Take a good sized sheet of paper and draw a circle in the center with a star in the middle. To the left of the circle and to the right draw four smaller circles, not touching each other. At the end of each row, draw a box. Put your initials in one box and your child's in the other. Put a stone in the middle of the circle. Then let your child play the game in the usual way, holding out her two hands, one with a stone. You guess which hand has the stone. If you guess right, you move the stone toward your home square. If you guess wrong, you move the stone toward her home square. The game is complete when the stone reaches someone's home square. Then play again with you holding the stone and your child guessing.

Homemade Calendar

If you are trying to teach your child to get organized (which is likely to be a long-term project, one that some of us are still working on in adulthood), you might use a rainy day to make a wipe-off calendar.

Find a piece of cardboard—those boards that come in shirts from the cleaners are perfect or the back side of a legal pad. Let the long side of the board run from left to right. Make a line a generous inch from the top—this is where the month and the year will go—then help your child divide the board into a grid with seven blocks across and six blocks down.

SIZE WISE

If you are doing this with a very young child, use a bigger board because your child will prefer to make pictures rather than word reminders.

The only thing your child will write on the board itself, except for the grid, is the days of the week on the first row of the grid. Then cover the board with plastic wrap or, better, clear plastic vinyl adhesive like "Contact" paper.

Now, using a washable marker, your child is ready to print the month and the year and, looking at an existing calendar, put the number of each day in the right box.

When this work is finished, you and your child can decide what reminders to put in each box—school events, visits to family, sports games or holidays. You can also agree on chores like cleaning her room or watering the plants. At the end of the month, erase the plastic and start again.

Building

There are many specialty toys that attract our children's interest, but few toys seem to survive as long and to satisfy as many children at as many ages as good, solid wooden blocks, Legos, Tinkertoys, and other building components that have no rules. Both boys and girls exercise many developmental skills in unstructured play with building materials. Often, all it takes to get your child immersed for hours in play is spilling a box of blocks or Legos onto the floor.

If your child wants some ideas to start the design juices flowing, suggest the following: a racetrack with ramps and tunnels for small cars; a city on the moon; a tower as high as the sofa cushions; a fortress; a secret hiding place. Add toy figures and small cars to the floor to give variety to the play.

Paper Sculpture

You and your child can make your own interesting stacking blocks out of paper. Using drawing or con-

struction paper, cut inch-wide strips of various
lengths. Try these sizes—one-by-twelve inches, one-
by-eight inches, and one-by-six inches. Fold each strip
in fourths (in half and then in half again). Then bend
each section on the crease until it falls into a square.
Tape the edges of the square together with tape. Now
you're ready to make square building blocks with
open centers.

Your daughter will have fun arranging these lightweight and pliable blocks into two- and three-dimensional designs. She tapes one or two blocks to a sheet
of paper as if it were the foundation of her structure.
Then, she adds blocks on top and beside with tape.
We've seen kids build skyscrapers, humans, and all
sort of abstract designs this way.

Eggshell Mosaics

What can you do with eggshells, besides avoid
walking on them? Here is a creative use for the residue
from the breakfast scramble. Save shells from about
one dozen eggs. Wash them and let them dry on a
sheet of paper. Then set your child to work crushing
the shells by pounding them with a spoon. (She will
love this part.)

Fill two or three glasses or plastic cups with food
coloring (or leftover Easter egg dye, which works
perfectly) and water. Divide the shells among the
cups and stir until all the shells are covered. Let the
shells sit in the solution until they really absorb the
color—maybe fifteen minutes or so. Have your
child remove the shells from the solution with a
fork and place them on paper toweling. Leave them
there overnight to dry. The next day, she can design
a picture by gluing eggshells to paper, either alone

in a mosaic design or as a highlight to a crayon creation.

_____ ADDED ATTRACTION _____

As the eggshells dry, your child can do some tie-dying with the colored water. Using white rags or squares of paper towels, twist sections of the fabric or paper together and hold with a rubber band. Dip the twisted sections in one or more colors of dye and let dry. (The paper towel dries quite quickly. You can toss the fabric in the dryer if it is not drippy.) The result is hand-designed tie-dyed fabric or paper.

Clay Sculpture

Clay has diverse qualities of appeal. The exquisite, translucent work of ancient Chinese potters is one valued quality, and the work of a busy toddler, totally absorbed at the kitchen table on a rainy Thursday, is another. Clay and its more pliable, more edible, more cleanable sister substance—play dough—offers kids an opportunity to build, shape, and sculpt. (For play dough recipe, see Chapter 7.)

The simplest activity is flattening a piece of clay or play dough on a hard surface. Put some paper underneath to make cleaning up easier. For extra fun, give your child a rolling pin and let her roll out the clay. Help her find all kinds of objects to press into the clay. Your artist may try abstract art and then realism. She can poke or press toothpicks, popsicle sticks, and straws into the clay to make designs or standing structures. Buttons, plastic or wood alphabet letters, paper clips, bottle caps, and other small objects give lovely textural effects when pressed into the clay and removed. Cookie cutters are also fun for outlining shapes.

Then let her flatten the clay again and press color comic strips onto it. Remove the paper and amuse your child with the duplicated imprint of the comics.

Now have her take small lumps of clay and roll out snaky strips. These can be used to fashion bowls, vases, and pots as well as clay jewelry.

Sailing to China

You must use your judgment here and make sure your child is 100 percent healthy, but if the weather conditions are suitable, let your child go out in the rain. Nothing is more fun than climbing into boots and rain gear and heading for the gutter with some paper plates and paper cups and sailing them to China. Perhaps your child can spend some time in the morning making boats from small bars of hotel soap, paper plates, and cups.

Jumping in puddles, damming up runoff with piles of pebbles, and collecting water from the spout teach children how much fun they can have with very simple things.

So long as your children do not sit around in damp clothing and are dressed appropriately, the rain will not hurt them, and they will learn that bad weather is no reason to stop the world.

Tracing Stuff

Go hunting with your child for things around the house that can be traced—container lids, blocks, spoons, puzzle pieces, game parts, shoes. Let your child trace these items with a pencil on various pieces of paper. You or she can cut the objects out. Then they are ready to be colored and placed together to form a collage.

This simple activity teaches young children about shape and design while helping them to develop hand-eye coordination.

Scarfing

Your child will be blessed if she grows up feeling comfortable moving her body, whether it is dancing, sports or exercise. One way to encourage young children to move freely and imaginatively and to have fun, too, is to collect an assortment of old scarves, large and small, for scarf dancing.

Fill a box with scarves—chiffon things and flannel mufflers and silk squares—whatever you have in the house and can collect from others. On a dull day, bring out this bright collection and turn on some music. Have your child close her eyes and pull out a scarf or two. You might like to pull one out, too. Turn on the music and dance around the room waving the scarves. You'll both get exercise.

If this is fun for your child, add variations. Imagine the scarf is a beautiful snake and dance it through the jungle. Or imagine the scarf is a floating ballerina, an airplane, or even a high flying basketball player.

ARTFUL STORAGE

Store the scarves in a box your child has decorated. Of course, it can be done with paints or crayons but maybe for this purpose, the box could be decorated with old scraps of fabric and buttons glued in place.

Sound Engineer

This is a storytelling activity with sound-effects that requires props, but gathering the props is part of the fun. Look for things around the house that make different kinds of dramatic sounds. For example, you might put out a cookie sheet and metal spoon, a pair of hiking boots and a board wide enough for the boots, a clean can with dried beans inside, a pot with its lid, and a whistle.

Also find your tape recorder and a blank tape. Now you are ready to make a (hear the flourish in our voices!) Raaadio Story Hour!!

Start with a tale of woe and adventure. It might start:

"One day we were walking in the woods and all of a sudden we heard loud footsteps. (Put your hands in the boots and pound them gently on the board.) At first the sound was soft, but then it got louder and louder. (You know what to do.) I turned around and there was a huge bear. I was really scared but I stood perfectly still and suddenly there was a rumble in the sky. (Roll the spoon over the cookie sheet.) I looked up in the sky and huge rain drops starting falling. (Shake the can with the beans) and the bear put up his umbrella and walked away. The rain stopped and I knew I had to get out of this forest. . . ."

Well, you get the idea. Go through the story once with you both telling it and helping out with the sound effects. Then tell your child it is time to tape the story, and she will be the sound engineer. You will tell the story again, and she will do the sound effects. Turn on the tape recorder and do it. Then at dinner or bedtime, you can play the tape for others in the family or for your own pleasure. As your child gets older, she and a friend can do this together.

Puppet Show

Surely puppets were invented on a rainy day. Organizing a puppet show is something one child or several can do. Place two bed sheets over a table large enough for a child or two to crawl under. Arrange the sheets so they overlap, and a child can stick his hand out as through a curtain.

Puppets, stuffed animals, or dolls can be used for the story characters. Or, if you want to make this activity last longer, let your child make puppets first from socks or paper lunch bags. Then, of course, it is time for your child to write, direct, and produce the puppet theater.

BAG PEOPLE

An easy way to make good puppets with regular kitchen materials is to stuff a lunch bag with one page of newspaper to fill about half the bag. Twist the bag closed in the middle and tie a twisty-tie or a rubber band around the twist. As you are tying it, slip in a chop stick, a straw, or any straight safe object that is about 8–12 inches long. There, you have a puppet with a puppet rod. Show your child how it will look when it is finished, then let her make several puppet faces from bags that are still flat.

Famous Feet

If you are not intimidated by a little mess, we promise you will love this activity years later when your tiny child is bigger than you are. Tell your child about the well-known theater in Los Angeles, Grauman's, where famous movie stars are invited to leave their footprints in the sidewalk. Since she is a star in your family, it seems perfectly sensible that you preserve her foot print.

Pour about a half inch of tempera paint into a flat pan—the silver foil baking pans are perfect—with a bit of water. Put lots of newspaper down on the floor in all directions and put the pan in the middle. Invite your child to take off her socks and shoes and put one bare foot into the paint. Let it drip for a second and then quickly stamp it on blank paper. The paint may tickle but tell her to hold her foot "frozen" so she can make a clear footprint.

While the paint is drying, it is fun to let her sit up on the sink and wash her feet in the kitchen sink. When the paint is dry, help your child to print her name, age and the date on the bottom of the print. Perhaps she will want to cut out her footprint, paste it on a colored sheet of paper, and frame this personal stamp for grandma.

DITTO

Works fine with hands, too.

Pillow Pal

Surrender up an old pillow and inexpensive pillow case so your child can make herself a pillow doll. (Often if someone has been in the hospital for a few days they will come home with an inexpensive pillow that is perfect for this purpose.)

Tie the pillow in the middle with a ribbon, old tie or whatever is around. Glue or stitch yarn or ribbon to the top of the pillow for hair. Draw on a face with indelible magic marker or cut facial features from fabric and, together, glue or sew them on.

Now you must decide how to dress the doll—boxer shorts, an old T-shirt or lengths of fabric for a more glamorous effect?

TOTE TIP

An old pillow case, custom decorated by your child, also makes a fine carrying case for a stuffed animal at risk of getting soiled while dragged everywhere, a cherished "blankie," or clothes to carry overnight to grandparents.

A Few of Our Favorite Things

Good cheer for a dreary day is to gather one's most favorite things and photograph them. Invite your child to bring them all into the living room and arrange them into a still life. Take some time working with your child to arrange the objects with style. Maybe his favorite comics should be rolled into his favorite slippers. Do you want all the objects on top of a favorite blanket—or should it be draped as the backdrop?

Once you have it the way you both like it, take a photograph. If you have a Polaroid, that's ideal. If not, finish the roll and use a one hour or one day developer.

You may want to try two or three arrangements, photographing each. Date the pictures and save them. Older children may like writing or dictating stories about the objects to special relatives.

Mysterious Sounds

Want to have some fun with the members of your family? Spend an hour or so with your child making a tape of different household noises. Think about the whoosh of the washing machine, the flush of the toilet and the rain of the shower. Turn on the car, and then let it run. Crank up the lawn mower, and slam the front door.

You can add to the tape at other times. Maybe you will want to include the baby crying or Dad coughing or the crackle of the morning newspaper.

Then, one day when the family is on a car trip or you are spending an evening with grandparents or just after dinner, play the tape and see how many sounds other family members can recognize.

7

The Kitchen: A Laboratory for Fun

The kitchen is for cooking—but it is also for long talks, sharing secrets, being silly, and telling jokes. And for young children, it is a wonderful laboratory for learning, a place to practice small motor skills, develop science awareness, and understand measurement and organization. As children get older, they can really learn to cook, a skill that will benefit the child for a lifetime.

All the gadgets and activities related to preparing and cooking food and cleaning up can be endlessly fascinating to young children. Of course, precautions must be taken to make sure children are well protected from hot surfaces and hot food, electricity and poisons, and sharp or dangerous implements. But once the dangers are attended to, there is a world of pretend and purposeful activity in the kitchen. Almost every hour of food preparation contains some activity a child can mimic or share in.

Being cozy in the kitchen can be a satisfying way to unwind with your child on a weekend afternoon. Sample these kitchen activities, and see if they don't lead to your own KIDFUN recipes.

Beat It

The egg beater is one of the best kitchen gadgets for children. Put some water and a small amount of liquid detergent in a deep bowl and place it in the kitchen sink. Pull a chair up to the sink, give your child an apron, roll up his sleeves, and watch him have fun whipping up a giant froth. When interest begins to wane, let him experiment putting other ingredients in the water. Try sugar and salt and then add droplets of food color.

Have Tongs, Will Travel

A young child's motor skills are developing rapidly. As muscle coordination improves, your child will enjoy an increased feeling of power and control, and will be delighted to show off new accomplishments. If your child has developed the necessary dexterity, he will enjoy games with tongs.

Place some boxes (or plates) around the kitchen, one on the counter, one on the floor, one on a chair, and so on. In each box but one, place a small solid object (for example, a block, a battery, a plastic or rubber toy, an empty spool). Give your child a pair of tongs, and explain that the object of the game is to use the tongs to move all the objects into the empty box. See if he can do this with a decreasing number of drops.

He should become better and better at this game the more he plays. To increase the challenge, put smaller objects in the boxes. A sugar cube can replace the block, a ring can replace the toy, and so on. And the distances between the boxes can become greater. Use the kitchen timer to see how long it takes him and how long it takes you—or try it with the whole family.

_____ TONG TIP _____

The game can be easier or harder depending on the tongs. Ice tongs with spoon like endings are easier than kitchen tongs with flat endings. Barbecue tongs with wide bottoms may be easier still. Let your child begin with easy implements and then, as motor skills develop, work into harder tasks.

Face It

Sometimes, Sharla remembers, her mother would serve tuna fish with a green pepper smile, olive eyes, curly carrot hair and a parsley collar. Invite your child to be the food decorator and give an artistic touch to the mashed potatoes, oatmeal, or meatloaf.

Some healthful garnishes include: cherry tomatoes; slices of green; red and yellow peppers; raisins; carrots, cucumber slices; olives; peas; capers; and nuts and seeds of various sorts.

Just Desserts

The place to begin learning to cook is with dessert, and children love making their own contributions.

Puddings and Jell-Os are lesson one. With you reading the instructions, your young child can practice pouring and stirring and measuring. Once he has mastered the basics, let him be a creative chef and add ingredients to these desserts as they begin to set. Miniature marshmallows, little candy hearts, peanuts, chocolate chips, maraschino cherries, and canned fruits are conventional favorites.

Another dessert your child can help you make is cookies. Let him help you roll out the dough of a package of refrigerator cookies and cut shapes in it with cookie cutters. Older children can cut their own shapes with a dull knife. They may want to do abstract shapes or animals or bake their name in cookie dough. And then suggest they brighten the cookies by decorating with sprinkles, icing, or raisins.

Lunch Munch

Another good time for decision making is lunch. Give your child a few acceptable choices, let him decide what he will eat, and then let him help you fix it. It's not as fast or as neat to have a toddler spread the peanut butter and jelly, layer the ham and cheese, or count out the raisins, but it will give your child a sense of importance and a nice message about self-reliance. Little children can also help with ready-mix cereals and soups, scrambled eggs, and lettuce that needs tearing. They can set the table, lay out the napkins, and deliver the cups.

Kitchen Pool

Play pool—right on the kitchen table. And don't be surprised if older siblings, parents and grandparents get in the act.

First, make the cue pockets by taping paper cups at either end of the table and, perhaps, a few along the sides or at all the corners. (Tape the cup so that it is flush with the edge of the table or just a smidge lower.) Make the cue stick by placing a long strand of raw spaghetti, which will be slid back and forth, inside a plastic drinking straw. Use whatever you can find in the kitchen that is small and round like Cheerios, sunflower seeds in the shell or M&Ms for the "balls."

After your child practices a bit, you and he may want to devise a scoring system based on the number of tries with the "cue stick" and the pocket the "ball" enters. Children can do this alone or you can challenge each other.

Touch and Tell

Young children can easily practice discrimination skills with fruits and vegetables. When unpacking produce from the market, place four or five items in a paper bag. Challenge your child to feel gently inside the bag and guess what each piece is. After each guess, he removes the piece to see if he was right.

You can make this activity more dramatic by blindfolding your child and letting him lift out each piece to smell as well as touch. If he cannot guess right, you can cut a piece of the fruit and let him taste. And when the game is over, set him to work helping you wash, peel, and slice the food into a fruit or vegetable salad.

Vegetable Scrubber

After you and your child have been to the supermarket and it's time to put away the groceries, set him up at the sink to be the official vegetable scrubber. Let him rub away the dirt spots on the potatoes and rinse the apples. What about the carrots and radishes? Is he ready to rinse the lettuce and spin it if you have a lettuce spinner?

Chefs' Choice

When it is time to think about the dinner menu, let your child help. A white paper bag is easily converted into a chef's hat. On a large piece of paper, draw squares and write down in the top of the box the food categories for your meals—perhaps meat, starch, vegetable, dessert, beverage, or whatever fits your family needs. Then let your child help you choose what you will make in each category. Print the choice at the bottom of the box and let him illustrate each box with a magazine picture, a drawing, or dried food glued on. When the family is seated together at dinner, he can proudly "read" the menu, never suspecting all that he has learned about food groups and reading.

Tastetesters

Choose a cookbook with lots of illustrations and look through it with your child, talking about how various foods taste—sour, sweet, salty, bitter, hot, spicy. Later, play a tasting game by gathering foods that have distinctive flavors—for instance, try lemon for sour, chocolate for sweet, pretzels for salty, radish for bitter, mustard or pepper for hot, and chili sauce or ketchup for spicy—and put them in a basket or bowl covered by a napkin. Have your child put on a blindfold or cover his eyes, stick out his tongue, and taste a bit of each item in the basket. See how many he can guess right. Talk about how different the tastes are.

Then reverse roles and let him put bits of food on your tongue. He may want to add some new items—pickles or peanut butter, garlic and onions.

The Nose Knows

Continue exploring the power of your child's senses with an experiment for the nose. Set up a row of containers—margarine dishes work well—and put a bit of aromatic food in each. You might try ground coffee, vinegar, peanut butter, a lemon slice, salami, sliced onions, ground herbs. Put lids on the containers. Then blindfold your child and, one by one, lift the lids and let your child smell the container. After each guess, remove the blindfold and let him see if he was right.

When he has tried to identify all the items, you can change places, and he can test you. He may want to replace some of the foods with new items—perhaps a slice of fruit, a pungent cheese, and some loose tea.

Play Dough

Put an apron on your kitchen kid, and set him to work whipping up a fresh batch of play dough. Spread some newspaper or a large plastic bag (or grocery bags cut down the side and opened flat) on a table and provide your child with a large bowl, a wooden spoon, and a measuring cup. Help him measure the following ingredients and blend them together gradually:

1-$\frac{1}{2}$ cups flour	$\frac{1}{4}$ cup water (add slowly)
$\frac{1}{2}$ cup salt	$\frac{1}{4}$ cup vegetable oil (add slowly)

When the consistency looks right, he can knead the play dough with his hands. For variety, add food color to the water before mixing.

The play dough will keep for weeks tied securely in a plastic bag in the refrigerator. Pat a little salad oil on the outside to keep it pliable if it feels dry.

While you are cooking dinner for the family, let your child cook up some gourmet treats for dolls or stuffed animals or just for fun. He can take "orders" from play figures and serve them his play dough delicacies on paper or plastic plates. Making available plastic tableware, paper and pencil for place mats, "menus," "bills," and homemade decorations can add to his busy and creative fun.

BETTER SERVICE

Buy waiter order sheets in an office supply store and add to his imaginary fun.

Watercoloring

Give your child several measuring cups or small bowls, a pitcher of water, and bottles of food coloring. Let him experiment by stirring droplets of food color into cups containing different amounts of water. If he does not discover it on his own, help him see that he can mix red and yellow to make orange, blue and yellow to make green, and red and blue to make purple.

If you have old sheeting material or a white T-shirt, cut it in squares, roll the squares up, tie them with rubber bands, and let him tie-dye. In a pinch, napkins or squares of paper toweling will do.

CAUTIONARY NOTE

Spread newspaper or plastic both on and under the kitchen table and take care that any chair upholstery is protected for this activity.

Salty Pictures

Art projects in the kitchen can be enhanced by texturing them with salt. Let your child apply glue to selected portions of his pictures, and sprinkle salt on top of the glue. (Use coarse salt or table salt.) The salt is particularly effective on a snow scene, a beach scene, a furry-salty-tail bunny, a fancy salty costume, or rain outside a window.

If your sense of thrift is not offended, your child might experiment with parsley flakes, sesame seeds, pepper, and other spices from your shelf for different artistic effects. Have your child shake the excess salt off the drawing onto the work paper. If you like, you can funnel the leftovers into a small container for another project.

Vegetable Patch

Paste, paper, and some supplies from your pantry are all that is needed for this kitchen art. Provide your child with a supply of various dried foods, like beans and peas, rice, macaroni, popcorn kernels, spaghetti, and whatever else inspires you. Let him spread paste all over the paper and arrange whatever designs strike his fancy. He may then want to use one of the items to create a border all around his work.

Kitchen Construction

Paper cups are great for building. So are plastic measuring cups, margarine containers, and metal bowls. Let your child try his stacking and balancing skills with a variety of nonbreakable kitchen objects. Let him see how high he can build.

_____ KITCHEN SANITY _____

Set aside a low cabinet shelf or drawer that belongs to your child. Stock it with a few old pots and pans, some safe kitchen implements, some cans, and some plastic cups. Now and then change around some of the items on the shelf. When you head for the kitchen, direct your child to his shelf or drawer.

Kitchen Bowling

If we've got you hooked on kitchen pool, maybe you and your son are ready for kitchen bowling. This is an easy way to entertain an energetic toddler while you are both hanging out in the kitchen.

Find something in your pantry that is tall, steady and unbreakable. We looked in the closet and hit upon an empty 64 oz. plastic bottle of soda. Then find a few soft balls around the house. Nerf balls are best but tennis balls work. Put the bottle somewhere on the kitchen floor. Some distance away chalk or tape a line. Challenge your child to see how many times he can bowl at the can and hit it. When he can do three in a row, tell him it is time to move the line—or the can—further away and try for the Super Bottle Challenge.

Try it yourself. It is fun.

Kitchen Gifts

While you are cooking dinner, your child can be preparing birthday and holiday gifts for the family.

Let your child design with crayons or markers both sides of two paper plates. Cut one of the two plates in half. Place the face of the whole and half plate together. Staple around the rim where the two plates join, and, voilà, a letter and note holder.

Use empty juice cans that have no rough edges for pencil holders. After you have washed and dried the can, your child can cover it and decorate it as a gift for favorite relatives. Older children can tackle decorating plain pottery mugs with nonwashable oil paints or permanent magic markers; make sure, of course, that you have protected everything for damage control.

Double Dish Washing

No adult ever found washing dishes as much fun as kids do when you let them climb into the sink. (This works much better if you happen to have a double sink.) Perch your toddler on the counter, feet in the sink, dish towel in hand. While you are washing or peeling, you can splash water on your friend's feet, pass him the plastic things to dry and generally, be silly and giggle without much loss of productivity.

Mush Gush

If you have no Scottish streak that weighs against waste of any kind, you might let your child try culinary creativity, no holds barred. One young friend of ours loved to bake cakes of his own invention. While his mother was measuring out the proper amounts according to a recipe, this chef was measuring according to some inner light. His cakes were never edible, but the challenge of actually arriving at a delectable dessert by sheer invention was good for many moments of fun.

As children get older, you can move from mush gush to real recipes. Find a simple recipe—perhaps a boxed mix to start—and ask your child to tackle it on his own. Make sure you are there to monitor at first, but let your child be "in charge." The sense of satisfaction that comes from serving his work, not yours, to the family reinforces independence and risk taking.

As your children get older, give them more kitchen responsibility. Help them become expert with one recipe—perhaps chili or macaroni and cheese or spaghetti sauce. Once they are comfortable in their cooking skills, you can encourage them to branch out.

Crayon Muffins

Here is a recipe that will please kids and recyclers equally. It requires that you and your child save bits of crayons, those that break or get worn down. Keep them in a coffee can in the kitchen. Then one day, when you are spending time in the kitchen and the can is at least a third full, you can make crayon muffins.

Have your child remove the paper from the crayons while you line an old muffin tin with silver foil. Fill the tin half full with crayons, and place it in a 300 degree pre-heated oven for about five minutes. Let the tin sit until it is cool. The colors will blend together and your child will be able to create multicolored art with only one crayon.

Did You Hear That?

This KIDFUN activity demands concentration, coordination, and good listening and is an interesting challenge to a little guy. Place three marbles in an empty pot, and challenge your child to walk around the kitchen making as little noise as possible. Whenever you hear the marbles, ask "Did You Hear That?"

Try this yourself to find out how difficult it is to transverse the kitchen without a sound.

Culinabulary

Put a sheet of lined paper on the refrigerator and write "Culinabulary" on the top. This is where your older child can keep track of kitchen words and skills he has mastered. Make the first word "culinary" so you can explain the title. Then, as you are using various cooking methods or making different kinds of food, from time to time stop to explain to your child what a particular word means and let him get involved in the cutting and stirring. When the cooking is done, let him write his newest achievement on the list. Ultimately, his list might read: "Saute; dice; souffle; pare; poach; whisk; braise; glaze." Oh, yes, how could we forget "defrost."

If, as your child gets older still and masters the techniques as well as the words, maybe you can give up cooking.

Counting

The kitchen is a great place to learn counting and basic math skills, and the teaching tool is cereal. In three plastic bowls, put three different cereals. This works best if one is a Cheerio shaped cereal, one is a small square like mini shredded wheats and the last is a flake cereal like Corn Flakes. Now you can let your child try his hand at "math homework." First, he might count out four Cheerios. Depending on age he can count out five shredded wheats or add to the four Cheerios three Shredded Wheats and two Corn Flakes for how many pieces of cereal? If you took away one Cheerio, one Shredded Wheat and one Corn Flake, that is nine take away three, how much would it be? Adjust the tasks to your child's level of ability.

Choices for Chores

H ousehold chores are no longer the private preserve of one family member. In busy families, everyone must pitch in and help with never-ending domestic responsibilities. Young children are not exempt. When children understand early on that they must help with the work, family life is easier, and the chores are done more quickly and with less friction.

The suggestions in "Choices for Chores" are designed to accustom children to household responsibility by beginning with activities that are fun but also rewarding, because the child needs to feel she has really contributed to the work that needs to be done.

Praise, of course, is a much better motivator than criticism, even "constructive" criticism. For many children it is easier to avoid a job than to hear how they might have done it better, so focus hard on the positives. The most useful kind of praise for young children is not general testimony to their goodness —"Sally, you are Mommy's best helper!" or "George, thank you so much for being so helpful!"—but calling specific attention to real accomplishments: "Jane, I feel so proud of you when you do a good job of picking up the toys like this" or "I am lucky to have a son who put away everyone's socks so well" or "Thank you for finishing the whole job without stopping."

We can be so eager to praise our children that sometimes we praise them for things they know they haven't really accomplished. There is a danger to this.

If your child decides your praise is the result of his special relationship to you and not really the result of his own effort, the praise you do give that is well-deserved may be discounted. Give love freely and unstintingly. Give praise when your child does something well or diligently.

When a child is especially competent and there is much to be done, there can be a tendency to add one too many responsibilities, and the child is left feeling bad about the last undone task instead of the successes beforehand. Aim to give your child tasks that fit with both abilities and attention span.

Color Sort

Even small children can help sort laundry if you use our neighbors' family secret: the color sort. Each person in the family selects a permanent marker of a different color. On the inside label of all her clothing or the bottom of her socks, her color is dotted.

An older child might make a chart to hang in the laundry room listing each person according to color.

When it is time to sort laundry, a child can be asked to find all the clothes with green dots or to gather all the socks with red dots and then black dots.

Any family with a multiplicity of white underpants, white socks, and blue jeans will find this a boon.

I.D. It

Name stamps are not very costly, and your child may be delighted to be appointed the family stamper. Stamping toys, books, equipment, and shoes as well as socks gives kids a nice sense of ownership and makes the house better organized. Everyone will know whose socks were left in the family room the night before.

Job Jar

With young children, have a special job jar from which they must choose jobs while you are doing your household jobs. Once a week, sit down with your child and fill out slips of paper with the jobs your child can do on her own. These can include traditional jobs like making the bed, picking up blocks, emptying the wastebasket, putting away the silverware from the dishwasher, setting the table, clearing the table, and dusting. For variety, add new jobs each week. These might include washing the side view mirror on the car, cleaning a drawer, sharpening pencils, sweeping the patio, or dusting a shelf of books.

As children get older, the whole family can share in the same job jar. When children are young, it is better for them to have their own, age-appropriate tasks.

HELPER'S HELPER

If your child is in the care of a housekeeper during the day, talk with your housekeeper about a job jar she and your child can use together.

Two by Two

The best way to teach children how to become proficient in anything is to model the desired behavior for them and praise whatever they do right. So team up with your child on tasks that work better with four hands than two: changing bed linens, moving furniture, scrubbing outdoor furniture, folding laundry.

Sometimes it is easier to do a job yourself than suffer help. Smeared car windows or spoons in the knife compartment may initially result from a child's effort to help. Avoid being critical. Repeat: Avoid being critical. Your child will probably not do the job as well as you. You are not aiming for perfection here but for a growing sense of responsibility.

Hang-Ups

Designate one or two days a week for your child to be the hang-up person. All the clothes left on chairs, the bottom of closet floors, and the floor get hung up. She can count how many items she hangs up each day.

Reorganizers

Tackle the toys with your child as your partner. Talk about how if she puts away her own toys she'll always be able to find them. Let her work on making labels for boxes, shelves, and drawers.

Charted

Sometimes the written word is more powerful than the parental yell. A "Chore Chart" may be just the motivator your family needs to spread out the work load. Make your chart for a month or two at a time. List jobs vertically on the left and dates horizontally across the top. Assign each person a color and put a colored star or a colored dot by each person's assignment for each week. When the job is done, the person completing it can circle the mark.

Scrub-a-Dub

Most young kids love to scrub. On a nice day, fill a bucket with soapy water outside and let your child scrub down toys, outdoor furniture, plastic storage boxes, or just the patio. Inside, set her to work at the kitchen sink with a sponge, a toothbrush, or a scouring pad and something you would like cleaned. Play some music to accompany the work and praise her as much for the effort as the result.

Creative Storage Boxes

A great way to push the notion of organization while letting your child have fun is to paint some organization boxes. Shoe boxes can store balls, dress boxes can order doll clothes or army figures, and larger boxes can be used for books and games.

Let her paint the boxes any way she wishes. This is her chance to go wild with purple or satisfy her abstract urges.

After the paint dries, use a laundry pen to mark the boxes: Amy's Book Box, All Doll Clothes, etc., and put your child to work organizing her stuff.

_____ JUNKBUSTER _____

Have a box with each person's name on it. When stuff—shoes, toys, books, clothes—is left around the house, simply drop it in the appropriate box and let the guilty party claim it.

Family Files

Buy a wide folder with accordion pleats on the side for each person in your family. Label the folders clearly and find a permanent place to store them—on a certain bookshelf, a closet shelf, or a file cabinet. Use the folders to store family memorabilia. Children often have things lying around their rooms that are too special to throw away but have no place: birthday cards, favorite drawings, sports programs, badges, pictures, tickets. With the folders, there will be a place for your children, and for you, to store these good memories.

The Steady Job

Many families assign to children their own steady job, which is theirs to do every week. The young child who gets in the habit of making her bed every day will generally continue without much argument—and the quality of the work will improve as well. Kindergarteners can be responsible for putting the silver in the dishwasher away every day, gathering up the newspapers, scrubbing a bathroom sink, or dusting the dining-room table.

If the job assignment takes only a little time and the child is rewarded for reliability, the groundwork for good work habits will have been started.

Beat the Clock

As children grow older, they may enjoy racing the clock in completing chores. This helps them stay focused on a task and turns the work into a game. Let your child decide how fast she thinks she can complete a chore, with you making sure speed will not endanger either the child or the household.

Have a chart on which a child can earn stars or points for beating her time. So many points earn a reward. The reward can be money, a treat, a special event, or a reprieve from doing a particular task for a day.

Pillow Plumping

Here is a chore that your house can probably survive without but your child will have so much fun doing it that it is worth pretending it is an important household mission. Appoint her to be the official pillow-plumper-upper.

The official pillow-plumper-upper must go through the house airing and poffing and plumping all the pillows until they are their fattest selves.

Hide the Prints

A simple but useful job for an early elementary school child is to go through the house removing the fingerprints from the woodwork around the door knobs. Give your child a sponge and whatever all purpose magic fingerprint-removing cleaner you use— perhaps put into a spray bottle if it's liquid for easy spritzing—and send her on her way or have her move from room to room as you do. Tell her to fix it so that no police detective can tell who went into which room.

Book Sorting

Candidly, this is, in our domestic estimation, a make-work job, and, as a matter of both principle and practicality, it seems better to give kids real work that will be useful. But sometimes you just need to have your child be busy—either because you need to be working, too, or because you think your child wants the discipline of accomplishing a task. When that is the case, put him to work sorting the books on your bookshelves by size. It is surprising how many decisions must be made in the act of book sorting, decisions that may come with hardly a conscious thought to you but require all sorts of discrimination judgment skills by your child.

Car Wash

If you want to be smart about planning for the future, teach your child now how to do a great job of washing your car. On a nice day, go outside together and wash the car. Talk to your child about how to do this job well. Give him small bits of things to do. For example, let her get those dirty cracks on the dash and doors with a Q-tip or vacuum the floor mats with a mini-vacuum. The trick here is have your child come away thinking car washing is fun and easy. Over time, keep developing his skills and competence at this task. And then, one day when toddler becomes teen, you can turn the job over—unless you two have become such a great car wash team that you aren't game to split up.

Socking Away the Socks

One of the great unsolved mysteries of the century is what happens to the "other" sock. Or, indeed, what happens to ALL the socks. Perhaps, you will be more successful than we are controlling the disappearance of socks in your house if your child becomes the Sock Supervisor.

The Sock Supervisor is the person who must pair all the socks, first by pattern and color and size and then, if similarity exists, whatever coding system you use in your house. Teach your child how to roll the socks and, when the job is done, to deliver the clean socks to each person's bed or drawer.

Soil Sorter

Many of us put our children to work helping to sort the clean clothes. An easier task for a little guy is to sort the dirty clothes into darks and lights. It can be kind of fun tossing those clothes into piles without any regard for creases and folds.

Dustbuster

You may have already tried Ghostbuster and Junk-buster activities. Then, it's time for Dustbuster, especially if your child takes great delight in crawling under, over and around things. Put a "Dustbuster", that terrific hand held vacuum, in her hands and let her squiggle into the tiny spaces you have been ignoring and suck up the dust balls under the beds, under the tables and in the out-of-the way corners while you vacuum the more accessible spots.

Gardening

Growing and tending a garden is a joyous chore for a young child. Your child can have a small plot of ground with her own marker; or, if this is not possible, some pots that are hers to water, to fertilize with you and to watch over lovingly.

Gardens are a wonderful task for children because all gardens demand regular care—but then gardens reward us for our efforts.

9

Visiting Your Office and Other Workplaces

For many children, parents disappear each day to "a job." What happens at that job remains a mystery. It is hard for kids to imagine what parents do when they go to work and what kind of place they go to.

When our children come to work with us—whether as an adventure or a solution to a babysitting dilemma —they are learning more about us and about the world. This helps them shape expectations for themselves and feel safer about our daily departures. Talk to your child about what you do at work and what others do there. Tell him why your job is important to the people who pay you.

A special trip to your workplace, just to introduce your child to your everyday world, is a great adventure for him. The office or workroom is a place rich with entertainment for children. It is full of props that can engage children in happy and educational play, but you should explain beforehand that what he will find are not toys but expensive machines that must be treated carefully.

One way to help parents who must bring a child to work is to have a computer already programmed with some educational games for kids of different ages. You might talk with the Human Resources person in your office about whether the company would consider investing in programs that employees' children could use when they had to come to work. Little children will like simple number and spatial relations games.

Older children can test their multiplication skills, learn to type, and practice written expression. Typing tutors, which make learning to touch type a game, are a wonderful way for a child to make good use of time at the office.

When you have your child at work out of necessity, you may feel torn by the work at hand and the needs of your child. On these days, try bringing a timer to work with you. Set the timer for a specified period and tell your child that when the timer rings, you will be able to stop your work and take a break if you can work without interruption in between.

Whether your child comes to work because of choice or crisis, here are some things to absorb his attention and stimulate his imagination.

Fun Photocopies

Children are fascinated by the miracle of making photocopies. Begin your child's work trip by visiting the photocopy machine. Make a coloring book at the machine. Photocopy each hand. Photocopy your hand next to your child's hand. Photocopy several rubber bands taped to a sheet of paper. Photocopy a page from a child's book or some diagram from a report on your desk. Use whatever is at hand to make an instant coloring book. Settle your child at an office desk with colored pencils or felt-tip pens and let her color the just-made sheets.

Tracing Tricks

A desk drawer is a treasure chest of interesting objects in all sizes and shapes. Pencils, pens, rulers, clips, rubber bands, magnets, staplers, and erasers are just some of the objects your child may find in your desk. Invite him to trace these objects on paper, overlapping one on top of the other to make a design. Later he can test you to see how many you recognize.

Pencil Stencil

Little kids often like to stencil. If your office has any kinds of stencils, haul them out and let your child work with different colored pencils. If nothing is on hand, you can make quick stencils from manila file folders or the backs of tablets. Cut a variety of shapes from this heavy paper and let your child use them on long sheets of copy paper.

MASTER-MAKER MEMO

If you are having trouble cutting into the middle of a heavy paper to make a stencil shape, just cut a straight line from the edge to where you want the shape to be, then tape the line back up. Make sure you leave a wide border around the shape, however, for stability.

If your child gets engaged by this, he may want to repeat it at home on an old tee shirt or another piece of clothing using an indelible marker.

Older children might wish to stencil their own personal letterhead onto a sheet of paper. You can then run the original through the Xerox and produce a supply of personalized stationary for your child.

Calling Cards

If you have old business cards—yours or someone else's—on hand, your child is all set to make his own customized calling cards.

On either the business side or the blank side, your child can write his name and telephone number, making each card a unique effort. The next time he tells a friend to call him, he can give him one of his "calling cards" as a friendly reminder.

He can also use the cards to make his own card deck and even invent his own card game.

Clip Art

Paper clips are a wonderful toy in disguise. Your child can make jewelry for himself, his sister, or his grandma by stringing together paper clips. If your office has clips in colors, all the better. Those same clips are ideal for constructing highways and roads through which match box cars can be raced. No cars? Try erasers, stuck together with a few opened paper clips.

And when that stops being interesting, let your child arrange paper clips on a piece of paper and then trace them into a design ready to be colored. Photocopy the design several times before it is colored, and the clip artist is ready to do a whole color study: clips at rest in blue, clips at rest in rose with orange sunlight.

Find-a-Dot

If your office has a box of those small circular colored labels—they are often used to mark files—you can quickly plan a dot hunt for your child. While he is otherwise engaged, spin through the office and hide these small dots on various pieces of furniture or equipment.

Tell your child how many dots you have placed and see if he can find all of them.

Maintenance Man

Put your energetic youngster to work spiffing up the office. Ask him if he would like to earn a small amount of money going to work for the office and cleaning the conference room. Give him rags or paper towels and let him dust and shine the furniture.

Address Book

Your child can make his own address book. It will make him feel quite grown up to have his own set of telephone numbers, just as you may have yours on a Rolodex at work. Staple some sheets of paper together to make a book. Either print a friend's name on each sheet and let him draw a picture of the friend or let him draw first and you can print in the names afterward. Later, you can add the phone number and, if you like, the address for each friend. If he likes this activity, add relatives to his book.

White Before Your Eyes

Give your child a bottle of typing white-out and ask her to erase all the e's on a page of type. Or let her draw designs and then change them with the white-out.

Typed Messages

If you don't mind little fingers fiddling on the keyboard, let your child experiment with letter writing on the typewriter. Write a short, simple sentence and let a young child try to find the same letters on the keyboard. Or give him a series of instruction: ten e's, four th's, and six commas, followed by the child's name. Older children can type letters to friends or secret messages to hide at home under daddy's pillow or in sister's slipper. For even older children, bring along a typing book and challenge them to finish so many exercises before such and such a time. You may want to reward your child for meeting the challenge.

Files of Fun

File folders are good organizers for kids as well as office workers. If folders can be spared in your office, set your child to designing his own file folder system. You can label each folder with the heading of his choice, and he can decorate the folder or work on a logo for each heading.

Stampede

Use the stamps found in most offices to make abstract designs on paper. Encourage your children to experiment with repetitions, with abstract designs, and with different amounts of pressure.

There are no directions for this activity. Give your child hand-held stamps, a stamp pad, and plain paper. Your child will know what to do.

Bundling Bands

An entire box of rubber bands is a genuine treasure for most kids. Rubber bands can be made into balls, sculpture, and games. They can also be made, as we all remember, into very nice weapons. You might specifically caution your child about this last choice.

Just Like You

Duplicate a set of your work materials and set up your child in a safe spot to act just like you. A young child will love having a toy or unconnected phone nearby, a few different-size memo pads, magazines, directories, pencils, pens, stamping pads, and so on. In an office or even a factory, garage, or store, try to find a small area for your young person to "work" and pretend to be as official as you.

Telephone Talk

If the work setting can tolerate it, let your child talk on the telephone to a grandparent, a friend, or an imaginary playmate. One desperate mother we know used her credit card to call a grandparent in another city and have the grandparent read to the child over the phone while the mother banged out some necessary work.

Adding Up

Did you know calculators are made for kids who like to push buttons on a machine? If adding is part of your job, try to find an extra calculator and give your child a list of numbers to add while you are adding yours. Challenge a young child to do a list with one 1, two 2's, three 3's, and so on. Or, with school-age children, offer a series of age-appropriate problems and let your child work them out on the calculator.

Sorting Systems

An office, just like a home, has a list of undone chores. Perhaps your child can help out on his day at the office. He might straighten drawers, stack supplies, or alphabetize papers waiting to be filed.

Surprise Notes

Tear off part of a pad of stickum messages and let your child make up messages to stick up for various family members when you get home.

Copy Cat

Word processors and photocopy machines have made it harder for kids to know the joy of an old office staple: carbon paper. Carbon is great for amusing kids for good blocks of time. If you can round some up in your office, let your child experiment with the magic of double images. Or take a picture from a magazine and let her trace it onto typing paper.

Holey Art

Your child can make his own dot-to-dot activity page very easily by punching holes randomly in a piece of paper that is held over a waste basket. When interest in that wears off, he may happily continue to experiment with the hole puncher if you provide a manila file folder, a sheet of colored paper, or a piece of cardboard.

OPTICAL ILLUSION

A hole puncher can be used to add a special effect to art. If your child has drawn pictures of people, try hole punches for the eyes, as buttonholes on shirts, or designs on skirts.

Remember the Tapes from the Car?

In Chapter 1, we talked about having story tapes for the car and about making your own tapes of stories or sounds. NOW is the time to recycle those tapes. Bring them into the office, and let your child listen while you are working. If you have left them in the car, you might find them in the glove compartment on the way to work.

When that has run its course, suggest your child make his own tape by "reading" a story or telling a story for other children.

_____ OLDER FOLDER _____

If you have an older child with you, ask your child to do a helpful office task and make some tapes for younger children who come to the office by reading stories or telling stories on tape. You can leave these at the office for other parents who find themselves at work with children.

Graph-It

Graph paper is a great toy for a little guy. You can create all sorts of games with those itty-bitty squares and a box of colored pencils or markers. Fill in assorted blocks with dots for him to connect. Block out his initials and let him color them in, making each square a different color from the one before it. Or teach counting by blocking out grids of different sizes—3 by 4 or 7 by 8—and asking your child to copy the grid elsewhere on the paper.

To the Point

Do you remember that there was a style of painting developed by the Impressionists called Pointillism because the whole picture was created with dots of color? Let your child try out his Impressionistic impulses with a page or three of those sticker dots found in many offices.

The dots can be used for an abstract design, as the ingredients for flowers or balloons or letters or as the means to frame any pretty picture.

Then let your child try using dots from differently colored magic markers to make pictures.

_____ ART START _____

If your child is engaged by this, follow up with a trip to a nearby museum and try to find a painting done in the pointillist style. A French pointillist named Seurat is in many museums.

Key Hunt

Computers are here to stay, and that means knowing how to type is as important as knowing how to write. Young children can begin to learn the keyboard and have fun with the game of Key Hunt. The object is simple—to have your child find the chosen key with increasing speed. For little ones, you can start out by asking them to find the letters of the alphabet. They can be working on that while you are at your desk. Then you can ask them to spell out short two and three letter words. Next you can give them a stack of cards with different letters and let them look at the card and find the key. Then, for children a little older, give them the stack of letters and see how many they can hit accurately without looking at the keyboard. If your child is frustrated, suggest he play with a typing tutor and learn to touch type. And if he likes doing this, for sure give him time with the typing tutor.

As a reward for working on the computer, have your child type his name, then play around with typeface and fonts and give your child a sheet or two of his name in all manner of script and size.

10

Remembering Trips and Family Adventures

Children are natural historians. They want to know what happened when—when Mommy was a baby, when Daddy was a boy, when they were born, when Grandma came to see them for the first time, when their parents first met, and on through all the high points in your family history.

These stories give a sense of specialness and richness to family life. They celebrate the good times and serve as the basis on which to build more family history. Children absorb lessons in family values simply in the telling and retelling of the stories. But the past is not the only source of stories. As you have family adventures, trips, or reunions with your child, you can add to the family folklore by helping your child remember highlights of these events. Encouraging positive feelings in this way will strengthen your child's sense of family.

Here are some activities that can help your child develop a strong sense of family and of belonging.

The True Story

We know children love stories, and they especially love true stories. These stories are good to tell when your hands are busy working in the kitchen or the garage but your mind is free to recollect. Your children are likely to be delighted by events in your childhood—an adventure with your first bike, your first day of school, activities with your best friend, the day you got lost, the day you triumphed in some way, and so on.

Encourage other members of the family, especially older members, to share their true stories too, so your children can help preserve the family archives.

STORING TRUTHS

Keep a cassette player handy and record these story-telling sessions. Label them and save them in a special place.

I Remember

Pick a family event or trip that you and your child shared, and take turns mentioning the various things you did and saw. After you have exhausted all the details you can both remember, each of you can tell what the highlight of the trip or event was for you—the thing you liked best or thought most unusual or most interesting or funniest. The subject of "I Remember" might also be the subject for a book your child makes.

Travelogue

On days when you and your child have an outing without the rest of the family, encourage her to give the family a travelogue over dinner. Allow her to tell whatever she wants or remembers. You can ask questions to draw out more details, but it will be interesting for you to see what stood out in your child's memory.

She might accompany the travelogue with a display of mementos from the trip or drawings she made afterward.

Photographic Tale

When you have photos made from family trips or gatherings, have some extras made for your child. Let your child keep her own scrapbook where she can paste the pictures in an order that suits her. Together you can caption them. Your daughter might want to write or dictate a few sentences about each picture in the scrapbook as well. Now she can take out her own photographic collection and share it with others whenever she wishes.

PHOTO ALERT

Take or request pictures of family members your child does not see often. Put them in your child's scrapbook so that when you talk about these people, she can look up a face to help her remember who is who.

Many Thanks

On a family trip, your child may meet many new people who help make your trip enjoyable. One way to help your child remember some of these people and to remember high points on the trip is to write them a letter.

A young child can dictate the letter while you write it, and then she can add some illustrations. Involve her in the whole project—addressing the envelope, sealing, stamping, and mailing it.

This Is How It Was

Let your child look through magazines, newspapers, or brochures that you saved from the trip, searching for pictures that remind her of the adventure. Accept whatever your child selects. Paste the pictures on a sheet of construction paper and write under them whatever captions your child chooses.

COLLAGE COLLECTION

Have your child paste pictures on a large sheet of construction paper, trying to fill all the space, even if pictures overlap. Suggest he add objects to the collage to make it three-dimensional. He may want to add colored lines as well. The end result might be something you want to pop into a plastic frame box.

Can You Guess?

Play family charades, acting out people you've met or events you've experienced together, and see who can guess first. Take turns acting and guessing. You can act out everyday events like going to the hairdresser as well as major moments in your family history.

Postcard Memories

Encourage members of the family to send your child postcards, not only from trips but from the city in which they live. Save the postcards in a stack and, from time to time, go through the deck with your child and remember who has sent what from where.

COLLECT-A-CARD

Postcard collections are wonderful memory builders. Give your child a "postcard budget" on your next trip and let her buy an assortment of postcards. Write the date on the back and a highlight of the moment if your child wishes. Later, you can punch a hole in the top left corner and string all the cards together.

Grow Me Up Scrapbook

Do you remember the thrill of learning to write your own name? I have vague recollections of a thick black pencil my first-grade teacher gave me and very wide lined paper on which I wrote "SHARLA" over and over until the letters were straight, but those early efforts exist only in my mind. With my daughters, however, we have proof positive of their progress from scribbles to curlicues and flourishes.

In a plain spiral notebook, keep track of your child's signature progress. In our notebook we also have a fascinating chronicle of self-portraits and hand prints and dictated stories. Because of those stories we can recall, with a freshness that would otherwise be gone, our first trip to the Academy of Natural Science Museum, the highlight of which was a wonderful "lollop."

Kid Reporter

With children who are school age, bring a tape recorder along on trips and excursions. Let your child do an on-the-scene report, complete with authentic background noises. For kids who find this an adventure, encourage interviews with other visitors or staff—but don't force a shy youngster to do what you, but not she, consider fun.

Video Versions

If your family has access to a video camera and someone is willing to operate it, make a family movie. Have your children take turns being the interviewer. Start off with an interview on what people expect before the event you are filming. Then, when the video continues, you can see how realistic the expectations were. Be sure your reporter signs off with names, kids' ages, and the date. And be sure, too, that this is the fun it is meant to be and not too serious a production in which people can run the risk of being "wrong."

Holiday Decorations

The stuff of family vacations can often be used to make very personal Christmas tree decorations. Shells, twigs, and grasses all can be used creatively in Christmas decorations. Family pictures can be pasted onto circles of cardboard, framed in some decorative way, and hung from the tree.

Memory Quilt

If you or someone in your family is adept with a needle, think about sewing a memory quilt. Keep patches of favorite fabrics—the shirt your son wore when he got his first tooth, a square from a bedraggled sleepy blanket, and another from a favorite pair of sleepers or overalls. As your child gets older, save patches from the tee-ball team T-shirt or the Cub Scouts uniform and sew them onto squares of fabric. Use all of these to make a memory quilt.

Your child can use fabric crayons to color on material—you press over the crayons with wax paper and a hot iron when he's done—to make squares for the quilt, too, commemorating special occasions.

Alternatively, on each family trip you might look for one decoration or memento to bring home for the family collection.

Hand Book

Some families have guest books and ask visitors to sign. Your child might like to keep a hand book instead. Your child's hand should be on the very first page. If she is right-handed, have her place her left hand, with fingers spread out, firmly on the page and trace around it with her right hand. Under her hand, you or she should print her name, her age, and the date.

Each page after that is dedicated to a different person, either someone your child has visited or someone who has visited you. After your child traces the person's hand, remind her to ask that person to sign and date his or her hand. Your child may want to write or dictate a few sentences about the owner of each hand, too. Paw prints belong there, too.

An inexpensive spiral notebook works fine, as do the pretty cloth bound journals with blank pages.

Teach Me How

Different families have different ways of having fun.
Some families sing, others play sports, still others have
certain family games. When you are happily visiting
friends or relatives, look for something one of the people you are visiting can teach your child that is just for
fun. Grandma might teach a card game, grandpa, how
to shoot bottle caps or toss a stone. Cousins might perfect your child's whistle or some dance step. Let your
child spend lots of time on the new activity, making it
hers so that, ever after, the visit will be connected to
this activity.

It is a great compliment to a child to have an adult
teach her something special that the adult values and
thinks is a swell thing to do. And adults are delighted
to know that children want to learn from them. If,
however, you see your child is becoming impatient or
overwhelmed, you can teach her how to explain that
she needs to take a rest.

Prime Time Taping

Young children are not very adept at interviewing
their grandparents or other relatives, but they like to
be interviewed. You can engage your child for the
moment and take away valuable family stories by
serving as "talk show host" with your child and a chosen relative. Turn on the tape recorder. Then ask your
child a question. For example: "What is your favorite
thing to do outside?" After your child answers, you
can say, "Let's ask grandpa what he liked to do outside
when he was a boy." A second question might be,
"Please tell all these listeners what your favorite foods
are." Then get grandpa to talk about his favorite foods

growing up and let your child comment on whether she likes those foods, too. . . .

Collectibles

Buying souvenirs is an international occupation, and kids are as susceptible as adults. How about elevating the act of buying junk to the art of collecting? Help your child pick out one object that she would like to collect. For many children, it will be stuffed animals or trucks. However, it might also be patches, stamps, pennants, dolls or T-shirts. Susan's son Seth collected elephants; Sharla's daughter, Hope, collected clowns. Sharla's husband, Barry, still collects baseball caps and has hundreds of them. With each family trip, add a special item to the collection.

Rooting

If you and your child are visiting a place you like very much and want to remember, you can talk with your child about leaving a part of herself in this place and taking a part of this place inside herself. This may sound flaky at first, but memories are simply what we construct for ourselves, and this is way of building a memory for your child.

Find a place that you like—a spot in a park or a relative's yard or a corner of an amusement park—and stand there together. Tell your child to shut her eyes and think about sending some of her special energy down through her feet and into the ground beneath her. Invite her to tell the ground that is feeling her energy how she feels about this place. Then tell her to feel the energy and spirit of this place coming back up from the ground into her toes and climbing right through her body into her head. Now, you can explain, she has taken something of this place into herself, and it will always be inside of her; she can call it up in her mind whenever she wants.

Pin the Map

We hope you have already decided to find a place in the house to pin up a map of the world and another of the United States. If you don't have maps around, think about getting them and putting them on a kitchen or family room wall. If you prefer, you might choose a globe instead. As kids get older, maps are a terrific teaching aid. If, for example, the evening news discusses South Africa, you can find it on the map. If the soccer team from Argentina wins the game, you can find that, too.

More personally, your child can pin the places she has visited. You might also pin a small note on the border of the map that says, "Anna visits Aunt Harriet in Cleveland, June, 1994."

Refrigerator Album

With so much mobility, many of us live far away from family and beloved friends. Little children have trouble remembering just which one Aunt Cathy is or what cousin Jonathan looks like. Use the refrigerator as a front and center family album. You can attach pictures with tape or magnets or you can hunt around for the small frames with magnetized backs that are perfect on the refrigerator door. Then when relatives call or come up in stories you can bring their face right into view. It is especially good if you have photos with your child and the person you want to remember together.

Feel It

Mostly, we remember people and places and things. But we can also help our children to develop their sense of self esteem by remembering satisfying emotions as well. So much of good parenting is helping our kids to believe in themselves. If they can hold on to their moments of success and pleasure, joy and accomplishment, they are likely to feel good about themselves as adults. One way to do this is to tell your child to "take a picture" in her head of a positive moment. Help her stop and capture in her mind's eye just what she is wearing and what is happening and, most especially, how she is feeling.

Later on, in a different kind of moment, you can suggest to her she call up that picture and remember how she was feeling just then.

Mega Memory

We have talked several times about remembering good times with the help of photos—pictures in albums, on the frig, in video cassettes. Here is one more way to snap a time into permanence, one that slightly older kids will like. Take a photo of your child from her trip and blow it up into a poster. Let your child write a tag line across the poster and post it in her room. She can work on an entire wall collage starring her.

Stickered Suitcase

Both of us have had the happy experience of acquiring lots of stamps in our passports to show all the places we passed through. Kids get the same kind of pleasure as adults in pointing out all the places they have been. So find a small suitcase for your child that she can sticker to show her own adventures. If she and a cousin visit the zoo, she might want a lion sticker for her suitcase. Certainly trips out of town or even to the other side of town might be the occasion for adding a sticker.

SOLVING THE CASE

An old, hard-sided briefcase is likely to be much beloved by a young child. Or try some of the hard plastic boxes with handles from the office supply stores if you don't have a small suitcase on hand.

11

Hot Day Hints: For the Beach, the Pool, and the Yard

Water and sand have magical properties for children. On a hot day there is no better way to keep most children entertained than to let them loose on an expanse of sandy beach with a few buckets, a fistful of beach tools, a strainer, and a jug of cold water. Second best is a swimming pool, and even if you don't have access to an in-ground pool, you can create a little bit of beach in the backyard with an inexpensive plastic kiddie pool and a sandbox.

Here are some suggestions for adding to the simple pleasures of splashing and digging. These are activities you can do with your child or that you can suggest to older children who, inexplicably, seem more willing to engage with little children in the water than on the ground.

You will find that long, hot summer days suddenly seem quite short when everyone is wet and happy.

Follow the Leader

Have a group of children take turns being the leader in the kiddie pool. Join in the group and help out with suggestions that bring splashes and giggles. The leader might walk like a duck, paddle like a dog, or float on his back.

Chalk-In

When you are stocking up on summer supplies, buy some large poster chalk (this is the very *fat* chalk). Let your child and his friends decorate the driveway or sidewalk with chalk. Give them buckets of water or the hose to wash off one creation and make room for another.

If there are several kids, divide the drawing area into large squares and let each child have his own cement canvas. Or teach the kids hopscotch or other sidewalk games you played as a child.

If your child says, "What should I draw?" suggest a giant that stretches the whole length of the driveway or a garden with clouds and trees and sky or a super-highway with all kinds of cars and trucks and trains.

Cool Kid

Okay, it's a really hot day and there is no chance of finding a body of water, even one three feet wide, for relief. Your child is complaining that it is hot—and he's right. Take a spread and go outside under a tree. Take along an ice bucket filled with ice.

Have your child stretch out on the cloth like a fallen angel and tell him to look up at the sky but focus on the way his body is going to feel. Then take an ice cube and run it lightly along the bottoms of his feet. Run the ice on the insides of his wrists and elbows, too. If he likes the sensation, you can play around with the different feelings he gets from ice on different parts of his body. How does it feel on the back of his neck? What about on his tummy?

Then get your child to ice your feet, too. You will both feel like cool kids in no time.

Cloud Gazing

When it's too hot to move, don't. Stretch out in a shady spot and, laying side by side, look up at the sky and talk about what you see.

Channel Ball

Near the water's edge, where the sand is flat and wet, make a channel by placing sticks in two vertical rows about a foot apart. Sit at opposite ends of this channel and roll a ball through it to each other. Keep making the channel longer to see how far you can roll the ball. Experiment with ways to construct the channel to make the ball go faster or have a more complicated path.

Buried Treasure

Designate a particular small area as the playing field for this game. One player hides a distinguishable shell or other small object just below the surface of the sand (and everyone else must not peek) and smooths the sand over the buried treasure. He then counts slowly while the other player(s) pokes around in the sand with a popsicle stick to find the object. Children can take turns hiding and hunting—or you can hide a few objects and let everyone look at once.

Sand Artist

Flatten the surface of the sand and wet it to provide your child with a perfect drawing board. He can use a stick or rod to create his pictures. Mistakes can be erased in a minute. He can also practice writing letters and numbers in the sand.

Sand Bowling

Dig six holes in the sand to form a triangle, with the base of three holes toward you. Stand a few feet away and take turns rolling a ball toward the holes. You score three points if your ball goes in the single top hole, two points if it goes in either of the middle holes, and one point if it goes in any of the bottom holes.

Sand Castle

Help your child build an elaborate sand structure. Show him how to find objects that can enhance the structure—shells, stones, twigs, popsicle sticks, and bottle caps are all good. (Remember to take the man-made decorations to the trash can before you leave.)

Using big shapes for the base—like a large bucket of sand—will make it possible to build upward by placing smaller shapes of sand, formed from cups and margarine containers, on top. Bring lots of plastic containers of different shapes with you to the beach for molding. If you carry them in a net sack, you can easily hose them off or dip them in the ocean before getting in the car.

_____ CONSTRUCTION TIP _____

If your child is having trouble with shapes, set him to thinking about heaps. Suggest he make a small heap, then one that is bigger, then one that is bigger than that, and see how far he can go

.Sand Turtles

If your child has seen turtles or pictures of turtles, he might take pleasure in this sand sculpture activity.

First, take a walk together on the beach collecting shells. Then bring them back to your spot, and suggest your child sculpt a big turtle.

The sculpture is simple. A big oval mound is the body with a much smaller mound peeking out the top for the head and small bumps where the feet go. Once the turtle's body is packed down, he can cover the mound with the shells you found together, and the turtle will have his own shell.

Gold Diggers

All of us love to find unexpected treasures. You can give your kids the pleasure of prospecting for gold— oh well, copper—if you take a strainer or sifter and a bundle of pennies to the beach. While your child is playing elsewhere, scatter the pennies in a defined section and bury them in the sand.

When the time is right, hand over the sifter and let your child go mining for gold.

Kite Flying

This requires advance preparation, but the beach is a wonderful place for you and your child to fly kites. Inexpensive kites can be purchased at the variety store, but these are not sturdy items. You may want to buy an extra kite to have on hand as well as tape and extra string for emergencies.

With older children, a good winter project might be to build a kite to use on the beach, come summer.

Sprinkler Dancing

You may not be able to get to a beach and instead are heading for the backyard to cool off. All you need for a good time is a garden hose and a sprinkler. Young children love dancing in and out of the sprinkler. Set it low at first, then change the height, and if the sprinkler permits it, the direction of the water.

Wet Blanket

You probably hope your child won't be referred to as a wet blanket at birthday parties, but being a wet blanket is just the ticket for a hot summer afternoon. Take an old sheet or, better, thin bath towel, wet it and ring it out. Let your child drape himself in the wet towel or stretch out on the wet sheet as a way to stay cool. You may want to let your child rest in the shade on a damp towel at nap time in a very hot climate.

Pour and Measure

Whether at the beach or at home, your child can have a wonderful time pouring and measuring water, using a collection of clean household containers. Save up a collection of plastic squirt tubes, detergent bottles, spray bottles, jugs, and tubs just for this occasion.

Young children love water play, and it is especially

pleasurable when there is no need to worry about spills or accidents.

Body Painting

Get out the garden hose, some watercolor paints, and brushes and let your child body paint. He can imagine himself however he likes, wash it off, and start again. He may have telltale stripes for a day or two but, we promise, it wears off.

Painter for Hire

Give your young child a bucket of water and a wide paintbrush, and he can be busy painting for hours. He may decide to paint the cement by the pool, the sliding board, benches, toys—anything that will not be damaged by water. He will be fascinated to see how quickly the water is evaporated by the sun.

Sand Cookies

At the beach or at home in a sandbox, your child can have fun with a variety of cookie cutter shapes, making designs and preparing a tea party.

Water Prints

It is fun to make handprint or footprint patterns along the water's edge or on cement. Since they disappear quickly, there is a chance to be endlessly creative.

Your two-footed beach prowler might want to try making prints wearing different-size shoes, putting one foot in a bucket, or wearing flippers.

Shell Toss

Dig a hole in the sand and have a tossing contest. Set up a boundary line to stand behind and take turns tossing five shells into the hole. As your child gets better at this, set the starting line farther and farther away from the hole.

As a variation, put a stick in the sand. Each player finds a distinctive shell and marks it with his initial in crayon. Players take turns standing at the boundary line and tossing their shell toward the stick. Then see who came closest.

Beach Ball Flips

This is terrific activity for a crowd of grown-ups and children together. Everybody can have KIDFUN. All you need is a bunch of people, a sheet and a beach ball.

First, organize people into a circle while they hold onto the sheet at waist height. Count off, starting "one, two, one, two. . . " until everybody has a number. Now toss a beach ball into the center of the sheet. The "ones" must try to flip the ball OFF the sheet while the "twos" maneuver the sheet to keep the ball on top of it.

When the ball hits the ground, reverse the mission of each team. Cheer everybody on, especially the kids.

Penny Snatching

As your children become more proficient swimmers, they will enjoy diving for objects. Copper pennies are easy to see at the bottom of most pools, but any small, sinkable object will do. Very young children can enjoy wading in a kiddie pool for an object.

Yacht Club

We talked about boats in the bathtub in Chapter 3. In summertime, take those boats outside. Fill a plastic pool with an inch or two of water and proclaim it the local boat basin. Let your child collect all floatable objects and climb in with them.

ImaginIce

Building imagination is as important as building bodies and vocabularies. One day, when your child is baking in the sun, suggest he ImaginIce. Tell him to shut his eyes and create moving pictures in his mind to match your words. Then describe a very cold and icy scene in which your child is loving the ice and snow but feeling very cold. Ask him if he can imagine how cold the day feels against his skin and how chilly his fingers and toes are and how the wind is blowing and making everything colder. Tell him to see the trees with no leaves and the grass all covered with snow. Can he imagine himself being soooo cold and thinking how nice the hot sun would feel?

Sandbox

If you cannot get to the beach, bring a little beach to you. The most elaborate way to do this is to construct a sandbox with corner seats and edges high enough to keep the sand contained. (If you put in a bottom, make sure it can drain.) But your child can have just as much fun with several bags of sand heaped in the corner of the yard or even a single bag of sand dumped into a large container.

CAT ALERT

Be warned that cats like sand. You may want to cover your sand with a sheet of plastic when not in use to protect your child from animal waste.

Stone Soup

Very young children are so rich with imagination that the simplest activity takes on delicious dimensions. Stone Soup is this kind of opportunity. On a warm day, give your child a large plastic bowl, filled halfway with water and a wooden spoon. Invite him to make Stone Soup. First into the bowl must go a stone instead of a bone. Then your child will need to season his soup with what nature has to offer—a little dirt, blades of grass, twigs, etc. Ask your child what he can put in to give the soup some color. What kinds of leaves and flowers might add to the soup? Each time another ingredient is added the soup must be stirred well.

Of course, be sure he understands this soup is not for people. Absolutely no tasting, only concocting.

When the soup is done, let it get warm in the sun and then feed the hedges with this nutritious mixture.

BubblUp

You'll find in Chapter 13 that we recommend blowing bubbles as a good group activity, but it's pretty terrific on a hot summer day, too. Instead of making do with those little jars of bubbles, get out a bucket and mix up a gallon of bubble stuff by adding 1/4 cup of liquid dish detergent for each quart of water.

Take the bucket outside, along with a flat pan into which you can pour a small amount of bubble solution. Take along the cardboard roll from toilet paper or paper towels, the cardboard can from frozen juice with both ends removed, pipe cleaners that can be bent into circular shapes and anything else you think is good for experimenting.

STRAW VOTE

Drinking straws work if you are sure your child won't inhale the soapy water. You can also cut the center out of plastic lids of various sizes.

Then let your junior scientist experiment with what kinds of household stuff he can use to produce bubbles.

Hose Limbo

Haul out the hose and turn it on so there is a steady stream of water. Challenge your child to complete a series of feats. Let her jump over the stream of water. Keep raising the height of the water stream. Then reverse the game and let her slip under the stream. Now wave the hose and let her run through the water. Play hose tag, seeing if she can dodge your directed spray. When she is sufficiently wet and tired, spread out some towels and take a sunbath.

Scavenger Hunts

Planning-breakdowns are seldom welcome, but we expect them occasionally through the year. They are especially unwelcome, however, on vacation. If you are at the beach, for example, expecting to be out everyday on the sand and it rains, this is not happy news, especially if you are in a hotel.

What to do? Cook up some KIDFUN with a scavenger hunt, pairing kids and adults together. It could be real stuff that the teams collect or it could be answers to questions.

Sharla remembers scouring a hotel one winter vacation counting how many windows were in the lobby, how many tables were in the dining room and how many phones were on the basement level. See if you can find out where there is a red flower, a green chair and a bear? Where was the concierge born? What time does the breakfast cook come to the kitchen?

Scavenger hunts, of course, can be used whether it is hot or cold, home or hotel, little kids or teens.

12

Snowy Days

S now is magic. Can you remember as a child the excitement of waking to find a white-colored world one winter day? Let your children delight in the seasons and teach them early that snow doesn't mean they have to stay inside—so long as they have the proper outer wear to keep warm and dry.

Warm jackets, snow pants, hats, and boots are great items to buy secondhand, so you can keep a backup supply. When the first set of clothes gets wet enough to send shivers, it's nice to have a fresh change for a second round of outdoor fun. Especially helpful is a large box of gloves and mittens to keep the snowball crowd dry. Invest in equally warm clothes and boots for yourself, and go play right along with your child.

Sliding and Sledding

Sleds and snow go together like ice cream and cones. Have fun experimenting with different ways to go sledding.

Sharla's neighbors astonished her one morning by pulling their children down the street in last summer's bright orange, slightly cracked wading pool, to which they had attached some clothesline. Your kids will feel snug and special in their own pool as other kids go by on plain old snow sleds.

Another one-of-a-kind sled is a toboggan made from a large carton. Simply cut the carton apart, unfolding the sides so there is a large area on which to sit and one end to fold up and hold onto for support. This is a lightweight sled and easy for a child and his friends to carry to a nearby hill and use together. And when it or they are too soggy to slide anymore, the toboggan can go into a trash can, and hands are free to play in the snow coming home.

Angels

No child should have to grow up without the fun of making a snow angel. Show your child how to plant his feet firmly on the ground and fall back into a soft snow bank, then flap his hands and legs in the snow, as if he were flying, to make angel wings and a skirt. Then help him get up carefully so as not to disturb his angel shape. Fresh snow has a wonderful, floating texture, and kids love to lie in the snow and float in the crispness of a sunny winter day.

If angels are an old trick in your family, try making other body shapes, which resemble different animals. Maybe your son can figure out how to lie on his side and bend one arm to make an elephant trunk, or he can get on all fours to resemble horse's legs in the snow.

Snow Creatures

Everyone makes snowmen, but how about snow ladies, snow kids, snow dogs, cats, and turtles? This activity is great with a few people working together to build an entire family or menagerie of snow creatures.

For an added effect to delight those driving by, dress up your snow creatures with props. A hat and a scarf is traditional on your snowman, but how about a babushka (head scarf) or big hat for a snow girl? Maybe she should have a kitchen apron and a wooden spoon. If you are thrift-shop shopping, buy a few very inexpensive items to keep just to dress up snow people after the next big snowstorm.

If you are playing in the snow with very little people, make your snow people little too, so you don't tire out your tot. Or try making a snow turtle by mounding a shell-shaped body and adding four little feet, a head, and a tail.

Snow Sculptures

There are many other ways to shape snow besides making snow people. Encourage your child to think of snow as clay and to use it creatively to sculpt imaginative objects. Kitchen molds, plastic storage containers, and pots of all sizes can be used to give the snow special shapes, arranged according to your child's imagination. Small balls of snow can be connected by sticks or toothpicks and made into different configurations. Show your children how to slick different snow shapes together by spraying them with water and making "snow glue." If the snow is very soft and doesn't hold, children can add water or put their shapes in the freezer to harden for a few hours.

Or you and your child can arrange a snow tea party for the birds. Make snow cupcakes and decorate them with bird-feed icing.

Mitten Matt

If your son or daughter wants to go out on a snowy day to play and there is no one around for company, suggest Mitten Matt. Take a mitten whose mate has gotten lost—if your house is like ours, this should not be hard to find—and give it a face. Use buttons for eyes and red thread for a mouth or draw the face on with marker. Now your toddler is ready to take Mitten Matt outside and teach him how to play in the snow.

Snow Art

Some snow days are beautiful—but some are too cold and grim to want to spend much time outside. Instead, let your child create a warmer, drier snow scene inside. Here are two possibilities.

First, invite her to draw a winter outdoor scene. Cut open a brown grocery bag and use the inside as a large sheet of drawing paper. Then, against the brown background, add snow flakes by dabbing bits of cotton or cotton balls into a bowl of flour and onto the design. She might even glue bits of cotton to the scene.

Then switch to sculpture. Cover a table with newspaper or cloth for "snow" protection, and get out a foil lined tray. Using clay or play dough, let your child build mountains. Suggest he make different shaped mountains—a tall, thin one and a fat small one. When his mountain range is done, let him drizzle white glue over the mountain tops and sprinkle with salt. Save one mountain and drizzle it with sugar and another with flour. Decide which ones are whiter and look snowier.

Snow Cookies

If your child is eager to play with snow but you need him indoors, think about snow cookies. Fill a bucket or bowl with packed snow. Working quickly, have him press the snow into cookie cutters and drop the shapes onto a cookie sheet. Put the cookies in the freezer and save for later to serve to dolls, stuffed animals, or imaginary friends. Your son may want to decorate his frozen treats with gum drops, M&M's, or sprinkles, just for fun.

Snowy Colors

Just for a change, let your snow take on Technicolor. Pour a little food color into a paper cup half filled with water. Give your child a few cups with different colors. He can drizzle the colors across the snow or fill the cups with snow and have colored snow for balls or shapes or snow-people features.

This could be the perfect time to give a science lesson on colors. Give your child a container of red and yellow food color and have him pour half of each color into a cup of snow. With a plastic spoon, stir the concoction and watch his delight as he realizes he can make orange snow along with red and yellow.

Target Practice

When it is too damp to spend much time outside, but your child needs some exercise, this might do the trick and help develop hand-eye coordination as well. Collect some snow to form into snow balls and freeze them. (If it is too slushy, make snow ice cubes.) Make lots. When they are solid enough to stay together (but not rock hard—if they are too hard, give them a little time in the refrigerator so they are not weapons), put all the snow propellants in a plastic bowl. Let your child stand on a covered porch or some other protected place and see how well she can do aiming at a target—it can be a tree or a circle in the snow. Start easily and if your child is successful, move the target to a slightly more difficult position.

FREEZER TIP

Don't put all the snow balls in one plastic bag in the freezer, as one of us once did. Of course, they will all freeze together and you may find you can't get them apart before they start to melt.

Fort Snowstorm

Kids of any age can have fun building snow forts, but this seems to work especially well for school-age boys. We have seen boys exquisitely happy spending dozens of hours working on the construction of an "awesome" fort.

Your job is to make sure that the fort's foundation is laid in a place where it can remain for several days—instead of the middle of the driveway or on the back steps. Try to steer your snow architects to a place that does not receive too much direct sun, or the fort will be in danger of melting too quickly. Some kids like to use buckets of snow to shape their forts; others construct large snowballs and smash them together to form a wall; still others just hop into the middle of a snowbank, hollow it out, and hide inside.

Probably the most important role for you to play is to provide plenty of hot chocolate, grilled cheese squares, and a continual supply of dry mittens.

Mazes and Tunnels

Six inches or more of snow provide the ingredient for snow mazes and snow tunnels. Help your child draw a maze design to construct in the snow on a man-made or natural slope. Once the maze is constructed, slick it down with water and give it a very smooth surface. Then run toy cars or balls on the track. A group of children may want to build parallel mazes and race objects down them.

For more fun, build mazelike tunnels in the snow for the same purpose or, for young children, tunnels in which to hide objects for hide-and-seek.

Igloos

When the snow is just the right sticky consistency, it is time to think about igloo building. Eskimos build theirs with blocks of snow over several days, but a young tyke may just dive into a snow bank and hollow himself out an Eskimo style house. The artistic child may enjoy drawing a design on his igloo with a stick. It could be an abstract design, a form of sign language, or a newly invented family crest. An igloo just the right size for a plastic doll is fine too.

Shoveling

Keep a junior-size shovel in the garage and let your child help you shovel the driveway or walk. If his introduction to shoveling is fun, it will be much easier to up the ante and make a serious worker of him in later years. You might see how far you can shovel in five minutes or how long it takes the two of you to meet, starting at different ends.

Flaky Day

Bring the magic of snowflakes inside by decorating the window panes with colored dollies or snow flakes. Tell your child about the wonder of snow—that no two flakes are ever quite the same. Just like children, every one is different. With older children, you may want to get out an encyclopedia and see if you can find magnified pictures of snow flakes. If you have a good magnifying glass at home, collect your own flakes to look at.

Then let your child add color to paper flakes and hang them in the window. You can do this even if you live in a climate that never sees snow. Wait until there are pictures of big snowstorms somewhere else and decide to import a little to your house.

Carpet Square Skates

What better thing to do on an icy day than iceskate—well, pseudo ice skating. Six inch carpet squares, face down on a linoleum or wood floor work best, but you can make-do with two wash cloths. Find some slow dance or waltz music and challenge your child to become a champion "house skater." Get him to swing his arms to the music and sashay around the room. Then, with you watching to make sure he is safe, branch out into backwards skating and figure eights.

Physical education teacher, Janet Mizopalko, recommends this for building leg muscle strength.

Cold Weather Science

Use the cold weather to help your child become an experimental scientist, exploring the effects of the sun. Give her two cups—clear plastic is best but paper will do. Then have her make two colored water solutions, a different color in each cup. Fill each cup half full of the colored water. Then have your child place one cup outside in the sun and another outside in the shade. Every so often, check the cups and see which one is beginning to freeze first. How long does it take each cup to become frozen? Does the water freeze all over at the same time or is there a difference between the top of the cup and the bottom?

In warmer weather, your child can try the experiment in reverse. Place the colored water cups, covered with plastic wrap, in the freezer. When they are solid, place them out of doors, one in the sun and one in the shade. Watch how they melt.

Snowy Mountain Jumps

When it is too cold to jump in the snow out of doors, but jumping is clearly required by your energetic toddler, make snow covered peaks in the playroom.

Put pillows or sofa cushions on a wide open floor with nothing that can hurt or be hurt near by. Cover the pillows with a white sheet and declare them your daughter's own personal snow mountains. With an abracadabra, turn her into a snow mountain lion and let her jump from mountain to mountain. See how long it takes this lion to flatten the mountains. Then let her build them up again.

Card Art

Save all those holiday cards that come in December for the next big snow and bring them out to entertain your child. She can cut out pictures she likes, mount them on colored paper and make "art cards" to send to family; she can copy designs from the cards; or you and she can cut them into zig-zagged shaped pieces to make simple puzzles.

GIFT LIFT

Some of these cards are perfect for recycling into gift cards by cutting off the cover and folding or cutting it into a gift card. Punch a hole in the corner to tie onto gifts. You can do the cutting and your child can tie on the ribbon.

Bubble Pop

When you get a package with plastic bubble wrap in it, save the bubble wrap or buy a large sheet or two at a postal center or office supply store. One day, just for fun, haul it out and let your child jump and hop on it—try it with just socks—and see how many pops she can count. This is especially fun when two kids are jumping together—or at a party

Summer Snowballs

Two imaginative children we know used to package snowballs in the winter. They would form perfectly round, tightly packed snowballs in various sizes and put them into plastic baggies and hide them in the bottom of the family freezer. Then, one hot summer day one or the other would remember to bring them out for water play.

13

Party Fun and Other Group Ideas

Many parents find that their children are more easily absorbed in play when they have a friend to interact with. But when the friend is multiplied, and suddenly you have a group, competent, coping adults have been known to experience a moment of panic.

Whether it is a rainy day and you have suddenly become the depository for local children or you have purposefully arranged to invite a group—a regular play group, birthday guests, or an ad hoc collection of friends' children—here is a collection of activities designed to entertain the crew. Enjoy seeing the differences among children of the same age and eavesdropping on their conversations.

Remember that children have short attention spans and little tolerance for sitting still a long time. Plan to intersperse energetic activities with quiet ones to keep hyperactivity from overcharging your charges. And if an activity doesn't seem to work, drop it. Don't force a visiting child to stay at something because you thought it was a good idea. In any group of children, there will be a wide range of maturity levels. Some children can sustain interest in a given activity while others quickly become restless. Let them wander off and play at something else.

If you are having a party for your child, structure the party so you do not feel overwhelmed by the number of children or the level of activity. One parent we know determined the number of guests by the age of the child. Sometimes, however, it seems right to invite an entire class of children so no one will feel left out. If the group is large, you may especially want to limit the amount of time. An hour and a half to two hours is plenty of time for young children to spend partying.

Parties are meant to be fun. A party is your child's chance to be a star, the center of attention for a little while. On her birthday, she gets to go first, have the biggest piece of cake, and sit in the best chair. While manners cannot be put aside, letting the other guy go first is for another day.

If you are stressed and harried, your child may pick up the vibrations and feel less celebratory. It does not matter whether the game rules are followed exactly, the activities are perfectly completed, or the agenda rolled out on schedule. So long as chaos and conflict are kept away and the children are absorbed, the party will be a success.

Come as a Star

Invite the child to come to the party dressed as their favorite star. You can keep it general or theme-oriented like this—Come as a Rock Star, Come as a Movie Star, Come as a TV Star, or Come as a Sports Star. Plan the party around the theme with table decorations, posters, video movies for entertainment, music and games. One activity could be a Parade of Stars as they march around the party to music. You may want to take snapshots of each "star" as a favor placed in a homemade frame with a gold star border. An alternative is to provide a box with assorted materials for costumes so they can become a star at the party—capes, hats, feathers, and whatever odds and ends you have can be the props. While the children are working on their costumes, you can help them with makeup.

Pizza Party

Food is a main ingredient in party fun, so make it the center of the party. Invite your child's friends to a pizza party, a pancake brunch, a hot dog barbecue, or a sundae special.

Regardless of the main course, the toppings are the fun. Provide an array of choices from which the kids can choose and let your guests be as creative and unconventional as their stomachs desire. Let your daughter suggest toppings she would like.

Carnival Time

With a little bit of advance organization, you can create a great deal of fun by organizing a carnival, either indoors or out. You might plan a bean bag toss, paper cup pyramid targets, some sort of balancing game, and magnetic fish (see "Go Fishing" in this chapter). One-leg races, tug-of-war, and whatever else you and your child can think of will round out the carnival activities.

Use peanuts, M&M's, and pennies for prizes. Give out prizes just for trying and increase the same prize for winners, and supply paper bags to store the loot.

HOT DAY CARNIVAL

In the heat of summer make your carnival a cool-off activity by adding water to each activity. Bean bags can be tossed into water buckets and paper cups knocked down by water pistols or a spray bottle. Use cups with water for balancing acts and play "Go Fishing" in the wading pool. Serve popsicles instead of ice cream.

Make a Movie

When your kids start outgrowing bean bags and wading pools, organize a make-a-movie party if you can get a video tape camera with sound. Depending on the number of children, divide them into groups of four to six and charge each group with developing a script and assigning parts for the upcoming "shoot." Have lots of props on hand: old hats, long scarves or fabric, bits of old Halloween costumes, and stuffed animals. Brooms or mops may also come in handy.

Allow only fifteen or twenty minutes to prepare. Then have each group perform for the others while you videotape the show. Over dessert play back the films. (And if you don't have a camera, just forget the video aspects and call it theater.)

COMMERCIAL ADAPTATION

A shorter, more focused version of this is to give each group a household product and let them make a commercial.

Showtime

If the children in your group are old enough, think about organizing a show. Have the children figure out where the stage should be and what kind of curtain they can use. Then help each child design an act. Some children may want to perform alone—singing a song, dancing, or telling a riddle or joke. Others may want to work on a group act, tossing balls as a juggling team, putting on a skit, or singing collectively. You serve as announcer, giving fanfare to each act and stimulating the applause.

Locomotive

The more children you have for this game, the better. Line up your gang, with each child holding onto the elbows of the person in front. The first child is the engineer. She leads the train, making a whistling sound, "Whoooo," to start the train. When she whistles twice, "Whoooo, Whooooooo," the train must stop. She decides where the train is going and makes announcements, and she decides how the train will move—by skip or jump or hop or run. The children can take turns being engineer. If you have a large group, you might want two trains.

Deep Freeze

Have the children spread out around the yard or playroom. Call out some physical activity for them to perform: jump, skip, touch their toes, hop, do push-ups, and so on. They must continue the activity until you yell "Freeze!" The children must hold their poses until you call out "Unfreeze!" and stipulate a different action. Vary the time between freezes to keep the game interesting. Don't have children drop out if they break the freeze but rather see how many of them can manage to hold every freeze or all but one or all but two.

Kooky Races

Challenge your group to a set of unusual races. For instance, they can have an elephant race (where they stomp like elephants and swing their arms like trunks), or a hopping kangaroo race, a turtle race (where they crawl as if under a shell), a backward race, or a two-at-a-time race. Let the children come up with their own imaginative ideas.

Rope Hurdle

Here is a simple way to create an exciting game of skill. On a soft grassy place, tie a rope between two chairs (or two other stable objects) so that it hangs loosely several inches above the ground. The children are to pretend they are race horses jumping the hurdles. They must jump the rope without touching it.

You can increase the height by pulling the chairs farther apart. When the rope is too high for a child to jump over, she can crawl under, but she must not touch the rope. Bring the chairs closer together and lower the rope. Let children decide if they want to jump over or go under.

Basketball

Place a trash can or a large box outdoors for this ball-tossing game. Give the children a large ball and five chances to toss the ball into the container. If the children can score each time, move the box farther away or offer a smaller box. This game can serve children of many ages if you vary the size of the ball and container and the distances.

If you have many children, think about having two containers and two balls so that the waiting time is shorter.

_____ PARTY OLYMPICS _____

For a birthday party with older children, recruit some other adults and set up several stations with a different activity at each station. Give each child a score card and let her move from station to station earning points for various levels of accomplishment. While most of the activities will probably require physical skills, include some concentration games as well. Give points for trying as well as scoring, and have prizes for every level of points.

Penny Hunt

Get a roll or two of pennies and sprinkle them around the yard, or inside if necessary. You can make the hiding places harder or easier depending on the age of the children. Give the children a set amount of time to hunt the pennies. Let them keep what they find.

With older children, you might tell them how many pennies are hidden and let them count what they find and keep hunting until all or most are recovered.

Bounce Like a Ball

Here is a good way for children to be wild and active without being uncontrolled. Invite the children to pretend they are various inanimate objects that you have at hand. Start with a rubber band; wiggle it, stretch it, shoot it in the air, and let it drop. Ask the children to imitate the rubber band. Follow, perhaps, with a jack-in-the-box, a bouncing ball, a slinky, and a coil of rope. If the children are into the game and still bubbling with energy, let them suggest some things they would like to be: rockets, robots, snowballs, or shooting stars.

Funny Face

To prepare for this game, cut a large oval out of felt. Paste it to construction paper or a large piece of brown paper. Draw some hair around it and give it a polka-dot bow tie. Then cut shapes out of felt scraps for eyes, nose, ears, and mouth. If you need more parts, add some eyebrows, a pipe, and a hat.

Tape the construction paper to a wall at eye level for the children. Blindfold one child at a time and have them stick one of their face parts to the oval. (Felt should stick on felt without any help, but if necessary use some loops of masking tape on the back of the pieces.) The funny face they make should be good for lots of laughs. When the game is over, leave the face up. Some children may decide to keep experimenting.

Go Fishing

Your child can help you do the advance work for this game. She must cut simple fish shapes out of various colors of construction paper. Print a letter on each fish so that together one or several simple words will be spelled out. Attach a paper clip to the body of each fish and put them all in a bucket.

Using a small length of dowel or some other suitable stick, attach a length of string to the handle, with a light magnet at the other end. Let each child have a turn at fishing and see if she can help make words from the fish.

Blowing Bubbles

KIDFUN activities can usually be organized with what is at hand. But if you know ahead of time you are going to have a group of children to entertain, treat them and you by going to the variety store and buying bubbles. A single jar of bubbles holds magic and laughter and happiness.

_____ SOAP SAVER _____

An excited child with a full bottle of bubbles is at risk for spilling. Open each bottle and pour half into a pitcher. That way, if someone spills, all is not lost; when the children are done, you can refill the bottles for another day.

Bubbles are an especially good way to entertain a group of children of different ages. Even teenagers can have fun with a jar of bubbles.

All sizes of bubbles can be blown, depending on the blowing instrument. Plastic straws dipped into bubble solution make tiny bubbles. Plastic container lids with a center hole cut out make larger bubbles, and pipe cleaners bent into circles make still larger bubbles. When the instrument gets too large for the bubble jar, pour bubbles onto a cookie sheet and rest the instrument on the sheet. Retrieve it with tongs and shake it gently to see how humongous a bubble you can create.

Homemade Bingo

This is a great activity for any size of group. Two can play just as happily as ten. Prepare some bingo cards in advance. Draw eight or nine squares on each card, and write a different alphabet letter (or number from one to nine) in each square. Make each card different. Then prepare many small cards with letters (or numbers) on them.

Give each player a bingo card and eight or nine buttons, bottle caps, poker chips, or squares of silver foil to use as markers. You or one of the children can be the caller. Pick a letter (or number) and call it out. You may want to hold it up and show it to the children. If they find the same one on their cards, they cover it with a marker. The first child to fill the entire card calls "Bingo!"

_____ TIME SAVER _____

Inexpensive bingo games can be found in the toy department of large discount and other stores.

_____ MIND EXPANDER _____

You can also play animal bingo, flower bingo, object bingo, and so on, using pictures on the cards.

People Letters

If it is time for active play, try people letters. Print some capital letters with straight lines (T, E, A, M, N, W) on sheets of paper, one to a sheet. Have all the children lie down on the floor. Pick one child to select a letter. She must then arrange the children to form that letter.

Pass the Ball

You and the children sit on the floor in a circle with your legs spread wide apart. Hand one of the children a large ball. She rolls it across the floor directly into the legs of another child. That child rolls it to another, and so on. Tell the children the game is to keep the ball in constant motion.

Nursery Rhyme Charades

Sing or recite several nursery rhymes. Then help the children dramatize their favorites. Each child whispers to you which rhyme he likes. Then you and he act out this rhyme while the other children try to guess which it is.

Older children can be given a set of props and asked to act out a favorite fairy tale or rhyme on their own.

Dancing Animals

Play various kinds of music—classical, pop, rock, whatever you like—for the children to dance to and encourage them to move rhythmically with the music.

Suggest they pretend to be different animals dancing to the music. They can be waddling ducks, lumbering elephants, creeping cats, running mice, stalking tigers, and frisky dogs.

Musical Chairs

This is such an old favorite that grandparents and even great-grandparents may remember playing it. Line up chairs in a row, alternating the direction of the chairs. Use one less chair than there are children. Beat a drum or play a record (or the piano) while the children walk around the row of chairs. When the music stops, they scramble to sit down. The child who doesn't manage to land on a chair is out. Remove a chair until just one child is left. Vary the time you play the music. As more children are out, you may want to speed up the game.

Humanitree

Turn your houseful of children into trees. Help them think what parts of their bodies match up with parts of trees. Feet can be roots, their body the trunk, arms the branches, and fingers the leaves. You be the weather elements, and have the children react. You can be the wind and the sun and the rain. And from time to time you can pretend to be a lumberman with an ax to chop down a tree. When you call out "Timber!" the tree before you must fall.

Storytelling

Just as with a single child, storytelling can absorb a group. There are many things you can do. You can simply read a fascinating story to children, sharing the pictures as you go. You can read a story and have the children provide sound effects. You can act out a written or made-up story, leading the entire group on a trek through the jungle or an adventure in discovering the Wild West, or you can, with younger children, engage them in story songs. Invite the entire group to act out this one, "The Tortoise and the Hare:"

Once upon a time there was a hare—that's a rabbit.
(Place index fingers above your head like ears.)

And a tortoise—that's a big turtle.
(Curve arms forward and bend down on all fours.)

The hare could run very, very fast.
(Bend arms and alternate fists forward quickly.)

But the tortoise ran very, very slowly.
(Bend arms and alternate fists forward slowly.)

One day the hare said, "Let's have a race!"
(Cup hands around mouth as for yelling.)

Get ready. . . get set. . . go!
(Point forefinger and thumb in gun position, moving arm forward when you say "go.")

There goes the hare.
(Alternate fists forward quickly.)

And there goes the tortoise.
(Alternate fists forward slowly.)

Suddenly the hare stopped. He looked around. He couldn't see the tortoise.
(Place one hand over eyes as if searching.)

So he decided to take a nap under a tree.
(Close eyes and pretend to sleep, possibly snoring.)

All of a sudden. . . he woke up. He said, "I forgot the race! I'd better hurry up!"
(Alternate fists forward quickly.)

Meanwhile, the tortoise never gave up and kept on going.
(Slow movement of fists.)

Until he won the race.

(Clasp hands above the head like a champion.)

The hare was very angry.

(Angry expression, with hands at hips.)

And the tortoise was very happy.

(Smiling, victorious face.)

You can tell the story a second time by asking questions and letting the children fill in the responses and the motions.

Murder in the Dark

This Agatha Christie style of game can be intriguing for a group of five or more elementary school children. Print the words "Detective," "Victim," and "Murderer" on sheets of paper that are folded. Add the same size folded sheets with no words so that each person in the group can pick a sheet. The "detective" leaves the room, turning off the lights as she goes. All the characters mill around, and the "victim" quickly falls to the floor while the "murderer" gives no indication of her crime. The detective returns, turns on the light, and with questions and observation of body language and facial expressions has five minutes to guess the murderer. Keep playing until each person has been the "detective" at least once.

Fashion Show

Of course, we are opposed to gender stereotyping. Of course, girls should play with trucks and basketballs and boys, with pots and sewing stuff. But experience suggests that dressing up has special appeal for little girls.

Fill a box with old clothes. Put in high heels and scarves of every color. Don't forget robes and shirts, hat, ties, jackets and purses. Let each child concoct an elegant—or avant garde—outfit of her choosing. It helps to have a "fashion assistant" for tying bows and stepping into high heels. You might want to provide a bit of make-up assistance, too.

Then have a fashion show, letting each child float down the runway to some descriptive comment. The commentary takes us back to gender stereotyping. This is a chance to tell the girls they are great—in every way and in every kind of dress.

As Susie Q. shows her most dazzling creation, the commentary might begin with a tribute to her skills on the soccer field or on the piano. Comment on how she moves with grace in every setting and every kind of dress. Or imagine Linda Lou, strutting in your gold heels and leopard bathrobe to the ad lib: "Linda Lou is as dazzling today in floating leopard as she is in her blue jeans on the playground where she is admired for being a super fast runner. Today, she has exchanged her Nikes for gold heels, but tomorrow you are just as likely to see her racing to school to read. Here's to Linda Lou, all around girl, interesting and elegant."

Make a Mummy

This is fun for two slightly older kids or a group of kids paired into twos or threes. The object is to turn one child in each group into a museum quality mummy by wrapping him, head to foot—with slits of course for eyes, nose and mouth—so nothing shows but his feet and his face. First one to prop up a fully wrapped mummy is the winner if more than one group is wrapping. The only equipment is a few rolls of toilet paper.

Sack Hop

Traditionally, this activity requires a potato sack—but on the likely chance that you don't happen to have a potato sack right on hand, substitute old pillowcases. With a group of kids, arrange relay races. With just a few kids, make the game to hop or walk from one point to another before a certain amount of time runs out. Then try it hopping with only one foot in the sack.

COMPLICATING TWIST

If hopping gets too easy but your kids like these kinds of movement games, let them try three-legged walking. Two guys stand next to each other, each facing the same direction, and you tie their inside legs together. Then they must walk the distance on these three legs.

Itchy Fishy

If you have enough children to form a circle and hold up a double, queen, or king sheet, you are ready for this. As the group holds the sheet waist high, they shake it slightly to make ripples that resemble waves.

Select one child to crawl under the sheet and tickle another child at the ankle. The sheet holders have only one clue as to which direction the itchy fish is headed—his fin. While the fish is swimming in the water, he holds up one finger, sliding it along the sheet.

When the fish tickles you, it is your turn to become the fish, put up your fin, and set up under the water for your own prey to tickle.

Junk Art

We first saw the mesmerizing effects of junk at the Boston Children's Museum where our children spent hours one rainy day playing with all sorts of leftover stuff. If you can't get to Boston, never mind. Save your own junk: paper towel and toilet paper rolls, bits of wood, anything glittery, the foam curls that come in fragile packages, soda cans pop tops, popsicle sticks, whatever happens through your house. Stick it all in a box so that one day when your child and his friends say, "What can we do?" you can pull out the box and answer "Make me some fabulous, interesting work of art."

With older children, you might want to save bigger junk: broken chairs, construction stuff, etc. If you have workmen around the house, ask them if they have any safe throwaways. Then let your kids see what they can come up with.

Hoopdedo

Hula hoops are a great invention. They affirm the power of simplicity. Besides learning to make them spin around your waist, they are great for all kinds of target games. Put one on the ground, draw circles inside like a target with a number in each. Toss balls for points. Or jump in and out of it. Or spin it around on your arm.

Our favorite non-hula thing to do is to tie the hoop so it hangs from a branch of a tree. Then stand back and toss a ball through it. Ping pong balls and foam balls are safest but tennis balls and small beach balls work, too. So do balloons.

Have a Parade

Kids love a parade!

Spend some time letting the kids prepare. First they will need music instruments for the parade marchers. Every child can work on making a drum, but some might want to put beans in cans for noise makers or string a bunch of pie pans on a rope or whatever else you can think of. Have some bells, pot lids and whistles ready for when the parade is about to begin. (If you hand them out early, you are going have a headache soon.)

Work on banners or flags to carry in the parade and paper hats, which the kids can also make. Lengths of fabric or scarves tied to a ruler make good parade waving gear. It will help to have some marching music on hand, but it might be fun for the kids to work on their own marching music to start off with. How about Yankee Doodle Dandy or You're a Grand Old Flag?

TOUTING A CAUSE

Maybe these kids would like to parade for a cause. If so, they can make posters to hold up on their parade.

You might march around the yard, then, if you don't have grouchy neighbors, hit the road and do the block before collapsing with a snack.

14

Take a Walk and Other Outdoor Activities

P arents of teenagers complain that walking seems to be a lost art among the young—but not the preschooler. He may like cars and bikes and hot wheels, but he still loves to walk.

Whether you have a destination in mind or just set out for a stroll on a nice day, a walk is a wonderful way to spend time with your child. With the phone and desk and household clutter left behind, both you and your child are free to notice the environment around you.

By being curious and aware of the world around you, you will be teaching your child to be an alert and intelligent observer. You will also be teaching him that there is endless diversion just outside any door. A bonus is the exercise of walking. If your child comes to enjoy walking and thinks of it as an activity for pleasure, it can become a healthy, lifelong habit. You and he may want to have a special, sturdy pair of shoes or sneakers for walking.

To make walks even more enjoyable, here are some ideas to intersperse with just walking and talking and feeling the sunshine.

Airport Hike

Many adults have discovered that when the weather is too hot or too cold, a good place to walk is at indoor malls. If you and your child are ready for a hike but the weather is dreadful, how about skipping the mall and heading straight to the airport? Maybe you will want to bring a book about airplanes or just discuss on your own how many different kinds you see. Airports are also great for people-watching, and they have lots of space for running and jumping and roaring like a rocket.

When the weather is nice, try visiting a smaller airport where private planes arrive and depart. Take a picnic lunch so you can sit in a nearby field and watch as the planes land and take off. Perhaps, you will be lucky and find someone there who will let you and your child get a closer look at the planes and, maybe, even let your child into the cockpit. Who knows—this may launch the career of a future astronaut.

LAND BASED OPTION

Instead or in addition to the airport, what about the train station if there is one in your community? These days, many young children never get to ride a train except in the zoo. Check the train schedule in your town and see if it is possible to plan a short excursion. Perhaps you and your child could take the train one way and a friend and his or her child could drive there to surprise your child with greetings, take your return ticket back and let you drive the car home.

Skyline

Look up at the tops of buildings, picking out rectangles, squares, triangles, and stair step designs. Notice, particularly, the pattern of the buildings against the sky. When you get home, help your child make a city silhouette. He draws the skyline pattern on dark paper, cuts it out, and pastes it to a sheet of blue background paper. Small squares of yellow can be pasted on for windows here and there.

TOWN TIP

Be explorers. Drive to a different section of town and take a walk. If a skyline is not in sight but close by, drive over and check it out.

Rockettes

If the sun is shining, the air is breezy, and you are in a silly mood, put a little dance into your walk. Swing hands as you walk and chant:

Left, right, left, right,
Aren't we a beautiful sight.
With all our energy, all our might
It's left, right, left, right.

Swing high, swing low. Change the rhymes. Add a fancy step or skip. Count your steps by four and kick high on every third step.

Step along to rhythmic counting. Count by twos and then by tens, and maybe fives, and when that gets boring, march along to nursery rhymes.

Sing Along

Your child may find walking more fun if you sing together as you stride along. Watch and see how the song affects your pace. Speed up with a marching song and then see what happens when you switch to a lullaby. Take turns choosing the songs you sing.

Clock It

You do the hiding. Hide a treasure in the yard and challenge your child to find it. This is a great activity for a child who is beginning to tell time. Bring a watch or clock outside with you and give your child clues according to numbers of the clock. For example, if you are standing together at six o'clock, you can tell her the object can be found just a few giant steps away at 12 o'clock or that she must move first to about four o'clock.

For younger children, you can use hot and cold, left and right, front and back.

First to See

Choose something to be on the lookout for, and see which of you spots it first. It can be simple, like a red car or a store that sells newspapers or a window with a plant; with older children it can be more esoteric, like a convertible car or a sign that has the word "you" in it or a person with a leather briefcase.

Variations on a Theme

When your child has had enough of walking and talking and even singing, try "Follow the Leader." The leader announces how you are to walk for a certain stretch—to the corner, the mailbox, or until a car passes by. He may suggest you will hop, jump, take giant steps, place one hand on your head, gallop like a horse, walk five steps and touch your toes—or nose—and so on. Take turns being leader and change off frequently.

Collectibles

Take a shopping bag or box with you on your walk to hold your collectibles. Look for interesting things to bring home and share with the family. You may find a stone that sparkles, a beautiful leaf, a fat seed pod, or a fatter caterpillar. Remember that what fascinates your child may seem like junk to you, but unless it poses a hazard, let him collect it.

When you get home, spread your discoveries out on a step in the yard or a table inside and examine them closely. Find a magnifying glass and let your child look at them enlarged. Let him show his treasures to the rest of the family that evening. Some children may want to start collections of special rocks, leaves, or anything else that intrigues them. Give your child a shoe box to store the collection.

Naturalist

Some kids—some parents, too—are bug resistant. Even if you are one of these, try to make friends with just a few of the bugs in the neighborhood in addition to the leafy stuff. Bring along a plastic jar with a lid (punch some air holes in the lid) and see what you and your child can collect. Then come home and take a good look at these tiny creatures with a high-powered magnifying glass.

This is great for kids and pretty sure to be interesting for any adult that missed this science lesson growing up. It doesn't matter that you don't know much about zoology or botany. For now, it is just enough to look and talk about what you see.

As your children get older, they may develop an interest in collecting butterflies or other species of insects. A company called Caroline Biological Supply can provide your child with all the tools for a young naturalist or check with the gift shop at a local science museum.

How Far Is It?

As you are walking with your child, pick out some object in the near distance—the fire hydrant, for example. Then count the steps you take until you reach the object. Then pick another object. Compare how far away in step measurement different objects are. Try to estimate how many steps it will take to get to a close object. For example, if it took twenty-three paces to reach the mailbox, guess whether it will take more or less to reach the trash can.

You can walk in regular paces to one spot, then turn around and see how many fewer steps you need if you take giant steps walking back.

ATTENTION, SPACE CADETS

With older children, take along a ten-foot tape measure and teach them how far a foot, a yard, and ten feet really are by doing step measurements first and then figuring out how many steps equal a foot. Pace off some distances in steps and then remeasure with the tape to see how accurate you were.

It's a Noisy World

As you walk, listen for all the sounds and noises around you. Help your child discriminate between different sounds. Go for a walk in a park or woods and listen for sounds of nature—birds singing, leaves rustling in the wind, dogs barking, people's feet crunching on the paths.

Then go for a city walk and think about the traffic noises, the sounds of fire and police and ambulance sirens, and the talking, shouting, laughing, and radio playing from people. Listen for rattling garbage cans, basketballs on the playground, tennis balls on the court, and. . . .

You might talk with older children about words—onomatopoeic words, which capture a sound in the word, like bees buzzing and balls thwacking and chalk screeching. Make up your own words to describe sounds you hear. What might you call the sound a siren makes?

How Long Did It Take?

Before you go out for your walk, examine the time carefully. Set the hands of a toy clock to show the exact time you left the house or quickly make a clock with a paper plate. (Write the numerals around the rim. Use a paper fastener to stick paper or cardboard hands through the center. In a pinch, you can make do with a straight pin.)

When you return from walking, compare the hands of the paper clock with the real clock. Figure out how long you were gone. Move the hands of the paper clock around until they match the time on the real clock. This will give your child an idea of how much time has passed. If you do this after each walk, your child will note that little movement of the clock hands means less time and more movement means more time spent outdoors.

Is it Hot? Is it Cool?

While taking a walk, talk about how things feel. Look for objects made of different materials. Touch all kinds of things and compare how they feel. For example, on a hot day you can touch the ground and then a parked car and compare their temperatures. Then do the same thing on a very cold day. Your child will intuitively understand that metal is a good conductor of heat, that dark objects attract the sun, and that earth retains warmth.

Describe the different textures of the things you touch. Note that bricks are hard and rough. So is bark, but it is a different kind of roughness. Find things that are soft and sticky and prickly and wet.

Reach for the Stars

In China it is common to find groups of people of all ages exercising outside. Nursery schools, housed in very small spaces with no playgrounds, bring the children into the courtyard twice a day for exercises. You and your child might decide to find a favorite outdoor place where the two of you can exercise together. Do simple exercises that stretch and flex the body.

For example, you might begin by harvesting a basket of stars from last night's sky. When you have filled the basket by really reaching very high on each side, then plant the stars in the grass by taking a star with your left hand and planting it outside your right foot, then vice versa. Then sit down in the grass, stretch your legs wide apart and see if your child can pick a blade of grass by her right foot with her left hand and then her left. Then add whatever else seems fun to you. This of course, will be at least as good for you as your child.

_____ TONAL TONE UP _____

Bring along a radio or cassette player and add music to this exercise.

"E" for Excellent Environment

Pretend you are sanitation chiefs, inspecting the streets in your neighborhood. Discuss pollution with your child, emphasizing how nice a clean street, lawn, or park looks and how they would look if people just dropped their trash anywhere at all. Walk along your streets and rate them by their cleanliness.

Take along a bag to pick up litter left by thoughtless people. Sing "Please Don't Be a Litterbug" (to the tune of "Here We Go Round the Mulberry Bush") if you like:

Please, please don't be a litterbug.
Please, please don't be a litterbug.
Please, please don't be a litterbug.
'Cause every litter bit hurts.

With some luck, you might be able to carry this campaign over to your child's room and inspire a cleanup.

How Many Whats?

Choose something to count within a specified distance. You might teach your child about a certain plant—an azalea, for example—and then count how many houses have azaleas in the yard. Or you can count how many people who pass you are wearing glasses, how many green cars are parked on the street, or how many restaurants there are on the block. Take turns naming things to count.

Wall Ball

This simple and very old activity has probably engaged millions of children around the world—but may be new to high tech city kids. It has lots of variations, but here are the two we remember from our own childhoods. Start with a tennis ball and a racquet. For a little guy, a badminton racquet may work better. Find a brick or cement wall and see how long you can bounce the ball off the wall with the racquet. Susan remembers spending most of one summer trying to reach 100 without a miss.

Another way of helping your child develop eye-hand coordination is to throw the ball against the wall and let her try to catch it on one, two or three bounces. Give her points for each kind of catch. You can invent other tasks depending on your child's skills and interest.

Keep a ball handy for your walks. Kids of all ages love to play catch. With very little ones, you can sit in the grass and roll the ball. As they get better coordinated, you can bounce the ball to them and then, finally, start slow pitching in anticipation of those days on the ball field that are likely to be in your near future.

Low Cost Housing

If you can manage it, a wonderful way for young children to entertain themselves is in a little house in the yard. While wooden houses are the best, you can make do until the next rain with a cardboard house made from a huge packing carton.

NEIGHBORHOOD WATCH

Keep an eye out for moving vans in the neighborhood. The wardrobe boxes that the moving companies use for clothes are excellent building material for little kids—and you can meet the new neighbors while you are scrounging.

Put windows and doors in the box. Cut the cardboard only on three sides so that they stay attached to the box and can be closed like shutters. If you are building a house, think about putting shutters on the windows. Once the house is there, all kinds of imagination games are possible. Children can have lunch or "tea" in the house, they can imagine all kinds of visitors and they can decorate the house. Let them paint it, inside or out. Give it a number. Perhaps they would like to give it a name, too.

Your children will likely get busy climbing in and out the windows and over the house as well as entertaining in the house.

Bird Watching

Why not join with your child to learn to recognize and name the birds around you.

Buy a bird book and start looking for different kinds

of birds. You can keep a list in the kitchen and check which birds you have seen when you go out on a bird walk.

Sometimes it's fun to make up silly poems or stories about birds you see. Perhaps, you and your child will decide to put a bird feeder in the yard.

Flying

Instead of going for a walk, go for a fly. Encourage your child to fly down the walk being as many flying objects as she can.

"I'm an airplane. . . I'm a butterfly. . . I'm a mosquito, whinnnnnne!"

Talk with your child about the different ways of flying. The airplane has a motor and makes a loud noise. The butterfly is silent and graceful and hardly moves in the air, while the mosquito zips around sending its high pitched sound until it finds its prey.

How do kites and birds, blimps and bees, clouds and cranes move through the air?

Kite Flying

If you have never flown a kite, we should warn you—it can be harder than it looks to get that kite to soar. It is also glorious fun. You will want to find a large, open place where you are free of overhead wires and have room to run. The beach is the best place but a large grassy field, even an empty baseball diamond works fine. Wait until there is a little wind and then head out with two kites and lots of string and have fun. Start out with inexpensive kites. If you get hooked, you will both enjoy learning about the many beautiful kinds of kites.

Windy Weather Special

Kids who are not ready for kites can enjoy the wind in a simpler way. Buy a roll of streamer size crepe paper at the drugstore or supermarket. Cut some streamers 6–10 inches long and attach them to your child's belt loops or overalls straps. Then attach a handful to a blunt stick and set out on your windy walk as a one person parade—unless you decide to tie on your own streamers.

Raking Leaves

If you live in a part of the country that has a leaf-dropping fall, raking leaves is a must—even if you have a leaf blower or a yard service or you live in an apartment and have to go to the park to find the leaves.

Equip your child with a junior-sized rake, equip yourself with an adult-sized one and rake up a huge pile of leaves. If possible find a chair or bench or something from which your child can leap, and let her jump as many times as she likes. If you want to get back in touch with your own childhood, jump a few times yourself.

Wacky Walks

A Wacky Walk is, of course, one in which you get to walk every which wacky way. Start with the Tin Man walk from the Wizard of Oz. (If your child doesn't know the Wizard of Oz yet, you might decide to rent this movie one rainy or sick day and watch together or read the book at bedtime.) Walking stiff limbed is a chance to explain to your child about joints.

Try the rag doll walk next. What else can you and she think of together—how about marching like a soldier, tippy-toeing like a ballerina, giant stepping like Paul Bunyan or navigating backwards?

This is silly and fun but it is also educational and body building for young children.

Building Body Awareness

In some parts of the world, people naturally spend time together dancing or moving with each other. Before we had words to communicate, we had dance and movement. In this culture, we emphasize words over movement. If you and your child like movement activities, here is another way to enjoy moving. This is best done outside, but it can be done inside, too.

Start by having you and your child sway together. Then ask your child to imitate what you do. Slowly— VERY slowly—move your body in wide, stretching, graceful ways—slowly raise one arm and then the other. Just as slowly bring each back to your side. Raise one leg and then the other straight in front of you. Then lunge forward, bending your front knee and keeping your back leg straight with the heel on the floor so you can feel your muscles stretch. After a few minutes, let your child be the leader. Then do a walk around, walking as slowly as you can and feeling all that goes into walking. Take big, exaggerated steps in the slowest speed possible.

Help your child to keep the movement slow by talking about feeling her arm push the air away as she lifts it, about which parts of the leg get used when it is stretched, about how it feels to walk so slowly.

Do this for a short time, then end with a Jump for Joy.

Blindfold Walk

One day when you are in the park together, ask your child how she would like to experience the world without seeing, relying instead on touching and smelling. If she is curious, blindfold her and then take her by the hand and lead her to a tree trunk, to some flowers or bushes and to other things she can feel and smell.

_____ EARFUL _____

While you are talking about using the senses, do another sense awareness exercise. Lay down on the grass together, shut your eyes, and listen for how many different sounds you can hear.

Learning to Look

Older children who like to draw will appreciate the chance to spend time with you sketching out of doors. Whether or not your child turns out a masterpiece, you will be doing wonders for developing her powers of observation. She'll begin to notice shadows, sizes, textures and colors.

Buy each of you a sketch pad and some sketching pencils or pastels. You might want to invest in two camp stools as well. Then decide what kinds of things you want to draw. Do you want to do interesting houses in the neighborhood or trees in the park or some of both—or something else entirely? Lamp posts, traffic signs, animals at the zoo, cars at the curb, a single flower in the garden?

At first, agree that you will spend five minutes on the sketch. If your child is still engaged, suggest you spend another five minutes adding more details. If she gets restless before five minutes, talk with her about looking and looking and looking to help her notice every detail about the object. As she develops her concentration, you can spend longer on each sketch.

CRITIC'S CURB

Remember—the goal is to have fun not to turn out excellent art. Too much constructive criticism can ruin your child's interest. On the other hand, don't praise indiscriminately or your child will stop taking your compliments seriously.

15

Quiet Time Activities

E ven the most energetic whirlwinds need quiet time now and then. Time out of vigorous play for calmer activity can keep a child from tripping across that invisible line that separates energy from exhaustion. And it certainly can help parents and caretakers do the same.

Consider scheduling quiet time just before meals and nap or bedtime to let your super-mover wind down a bit and ease the transition from play to more structured time.

There are many activities in this book that can be used to entertain a child quietly. Here are a few additional ones to absorb an active child in quiet play. Some of our favorites, like a juice and cookies picnic, are simple, almost obvious, pastimes that get overlooked because they are so straightforward and available.

The Disappearing Number

Using either playing cards or numbers you have printed on three-by-five-inch cards, you can help your child develop observation and concentration. In numerical order, lay out a sequence of four or five numbers and tell your child to turn his back for a minute. Remove one card from the sequence and move the other cards together so there is no gap. Your child must then identify the missing number. If he has some trouble, give him a clue, such as "It's after six."

Later on you can make the game more challenging by using a sequence of numbers but mixing them up and letting your child arrange them to find the missing number.

With older children, you can play a variation by letting your child lay out between five and ten cards. Have him study the cards for as long as he likes. Then, while he closes her eyes, you remove one card and rearrange the others. See how many times he can figure out which card is missing.

Follow the Maestro

Ask your child to help you put on a music recital. Pretend one of you is a well-known conductor and the other is a world-famous singer. Take turns at both roles, choosing your favorite songs.

Make an elaborate program introduction to your imaginary audience. Then ham up your performances. The maestro and the prima donna work closely together. If the conductor moves her arms quickly, the singer must follow and sing quickly. When the conductor slows down, the singer must slow down. Raised arms mean louder and lowered arms mean softer, and if the conductor crosses her arms in front of her chest, the singer must hold the note until the conductor signals a "cut" sign.

Newspaper Reporting

If your child understands that the evening news and the newspaper summarize what happened that day, suggest you and he do your own news report. Sit down together and decide what the Bobby Tribune or the Ellen Reporter is going to say today.

Write one headline and two or three sentences about your child's day, following his story lead. Perhaps he will want to do a picture for the story. Then you can post it on his bedroom door.

The process of thinking through the day and putting words to paper is likely to help him calm down and digest all that has happened.

HEADLINE NEWS

For beginning readers, read the headlines together, then cut out a pile of headline words and make your own family headlines or write headlines to match your newspaper reporting for the day.

Rainbow Cards

Here is a different kind of memory game for younger children. Using at least six different colors of construction paper, help your child paste squares of each color on one side of 3 by 5 note cards, making sure no color can be seen when the card is turned over.

Make sure you have at least four cards for each color. Now your child can use the cards to expand his concentration. Lay the cards flat, color side down. Now he tries to turn over two of the same color. Or he can play a game of Go Fish in which he tries to pair all four of the same color together or whatever else you and he can cook up with these Rainbow Cards.

With very young children just learning colors, lay the cards around the room and ask him to "Hop on the orange card," then "Sit on the red card," and "Put the blue card on his head."

Cards

An easy way to spend quiet time with your child is to play a game of cards. Young children are absorbed for long periods with the old-fashioned games of "War," "Old Maid," and "Go Fish."

Slightly older children enjoy "Concentration," the real-cards version of Rainbow Cards, above.

Lay all the cards out face down in rows. One person turns over a card and must match it with the same number or picture card. Each pair that is matched is removed from the playing surface, and the person who eventually gets the most pairs wins the game. If there is no match, the cards are turned back, face down, to their spot in the grid. The trick, of course, is to concentrate on where each card sits. Start with only aces through sixes until your child develops her concentration skills.

Still older children will be happy for a long time playing "Gin Rummy" with you and, perhaps, with older relatives in the family. You might also try checkers and Chinese checkers and, if you are a chess player, eventually chess.

BOOKIE'S BONUS

Have your child check out the deck to make sure it is complete by sorting the cards in numerical order according to hearts, spades, diamonds, and clubs. Then have him shuffle the deck thoroughly.

Shaping Up

Have your child sit on the floor. Give her six popsicle sticks or tongue depressors. Call out a shape—"rectangle," for example—and let her form this with her sticks.

A variation is to give her a pile of toothpicks and hold up a playing card or a sheet of paper with a number written on it. Let her pick out the correct number of toothpicks from the pile. Or print a capital letter and let her duplicate it with tooth-picks.

Puzzles

Take a large magazine picture or a colored map and cut it into large zigzag pieces to make a puzzle. (If you have the time and inclination, first paste the picture to cardboard or construction paper.) Let your child see how quickly he can reassemble the pieces. If he is a puzzle lover, as he gets older and more able to handle many pieces, keep a special table set up where unfinished puzzles can wait to be resumed during a quiet time.

Do What I Say

Understanding and following precise directions can be a tricky thing, because it involves interpreting words that deal with size and with spatial and numerical concepts. A good way to build up such comprehension is through games, which give your child practice in a fun way.

Draw a line across the middle of a sheet of paper. You and your child take turns giving each other precise directions for things to write or draw. Here are some examples:

Draw a big circle below the line.
Put an "E" inside the circle.
Draw three small squares above the line.
Put an "X" inside the middle square.
Draw a triangle in one of the upper corners.
Put a check under the circle.
Draw a line from the first square to the triangle.

Start out by challenging your child to get three directions right, one after the other. Once he can do that, suggest he try to keep beating her record. Go for four, then five, and so on.

PATIENCE POINTER

This is easy for you, but not at all easy for a young child. If you get angry or make your child feel stupid in any way, you run the risk of discouraging learning and damaging self-esteem. Applaud what your child can do, and do not be displeased by what he cannot do. In this way, he will want to continue working with you for the praise instead of trying to avoid your displeasure.

Deep Relaxation

This exercise comes from *The Centering Book: Awareness Activities for Children, Parents and Teachers* by Dr. Gay Hendricks and Dr. Russel Wills. "There is a feeling of balance, a feeling of inner strength that we feel when we are *centered*. . . a solid integration of mind and body," write these doctors in the first chapter.

The concepts may seem advanced for a little child, but the learning how to find one's center is a gift for children. It helps them in stressful performance situations and in dealing with difficult emotions. If your child learns this as a game, he will be able to use it forever.

Find a carpeted space where you can lie down side by side together. Tell your child to wiggle himself into a comfortable position and then close his eyes.

Tell him to feel his hands at the ends of his arms and how heavy they can be. Now have him make a fist and hold it tight for about ten seconds. Continue with these instructions, pausing a few seconds between each:

Now relax and feel how easy your hands are.

Think about your shoulders. Make them tight and push them through your ears if you can. Hold them tight.

Now let them go and feel all the tight feelings go away from your body.

Keep your eyes closed but open your mouth just as far as it can go, stretching it wide.

Now relax your mouth and feel how much better it feels.

Press your tongue against the top of your mouth and make your jaw all tight.

Now relax and let the good, quiet feeling go all through your face and into your body.

Now wrinkle your nose and make an awful face.

Now relax and make your face feel all good.

Now make your chest and your tummy and your whole middle all tight and hard and hold it in until I tell you to relax.

Let your body go soft and feel all the tight feelings slide away.

Continue with these kinds of instructions for the thighs, the legs and the toes.

Then talk to your child about feeling all relaxed. Tell him that if he feels any tight places in his body, he can take a deep breath and send that breath out through the tight place and it will relax that place. Have him take several more deep breaths feeling peaceful and quiet inside. Then tell him you are going to count backwards from 10 to 1 and all the energy is going to return to his body and at one he is going to get up and feel happy and good and centered.

Tape Talk

Sit down with your child and make a tape to send to grandparents, favorite aunts, uncles, or cousins. Before you start taping, talk over what has been happening with your child and your family recently that he will want to tell about. Make up a list of "Reporter's Questions" that you can ask each other as you make the tape.

When you are ready, put a tape in a recorder and interview each other, using the questions on your list to make the tape. When you are finished, play it back and then take a walk to the mailbox.

Art Portfolio

It is satisfying for children to see that their artwork is important enough for you to keep. Have an art portfolio in which your child can store his favorite works. You can buy a portfolio in an art supply store, but it is more fun to make one, using two large sheets of construction paper or heavy cardboard from the sides of large cartons. Cut two pieces the same size (unless you are lucky enough to have one very large piece that you fold in half). Punch holes along the bottom and run a piece of rope through the holes, knotting it with fat knots on the outside of each board. Now that you have made sure pictures cannot fall out the bottom, run a much longer piece up each side, about six inches from the bottom, so the portfolio can open up like an artist's portfolio without falling out flat. Write your child's name in very fat letters on each side and let her fill in the lines and decorate the portfolio.

Now and then, look through the work in the portfolio and let your child decide which art project appeals to him, and which he would like to try again.

Face Off

Trigger your child's imagination by dropping him into the middle of other lives. Take one of his school photographs or a home snapshot and cut out the face. Then as you look through magazines or picture books, you can place his face on top of those in print and start him imagining himself in other roles. Talk quietly for a few minutes about what he is thinking.

Your child will really enjoy this if you have a photo of you as well and you drop both your faces into new bodies. You may find your own imagination has some fun as well.

Scriptwriting

Most of us use television as a convenient way to entertain our children and keep them quiet. Here is a way to use television without turning it on. Talk with your child about her favorite programs and characters. Then suggest you write a script together for his favorite show. You can do the writing while he does the imagining. Help him along by asking questions.

Many children will use the outlines of programs they have seen, but you can lead them to explore new twists and turns of plot with your questions and enthusiastic responses to their lines. When you are finished, you might try acting the script out together.

Clipping Service

If you have a child who is learning to read, take yesterday's newspaper and ask your child to cut out three pictures that interest him. Together, think of a simple noun or verb that fits each picture. (As you talk about the different words that each picture inspires, you will be doing a great deal of reading and writing readiness work with your child.) Then arrange the pictures on a sheet of paper in an order that makes an interesting or a silly sentence. Make up a sentence using words that describe each picture.

If the pictures are of a baseball player, an airplane and a VCR from an advertisement, you might come up with the sentence: "My magic machine flies me to the baseball game."

Stargazing

This activity is simple but special. Poke holes at random on the bottom of a paper cup. Go into a darkened room or closet and hold a flashlight inside the cup and point the cup at the ceiling. The light will shine through the punctures and give you your own planetarium. You might try this as a nighttime activity with the whole family and end up telling stories.

Zoot Shoot

If you are working in the kitchen or the office, this absorbing activity will cause your child to quiet down and focus. The danger—and the pleasure—is that you, too, may get hooked in and never finish the chore that brought you to the kitchen in the first place. See how many times you can shoot an object, using your fingers, across a table, touching the table edge but not falling off the table. Use a plastic object that slides easily—an empty margarine container works fine; try it, too, with a penny or a quarter.

For young children, to make the game easier, you might draw or tape some lines near the edge to create "almost zones" or allow the child three chances if reaching across the table seems too hard in one flick.

Mystery Box

One rainy day, make a mystery box to keep around the house. Take a square shaped gift box with a lid and cut two circles, large enough for your child's hands to fit through, on opposite sides of the box. Cut the openings so that a flap stays attached to the box at the top of the opening. Have your child decorate the box to make it really snazzy.

Now, from time to time, place one of more objects inside the box. Challenge your child to figure out what is in the box. At first, let him put one hand inside the box and one resting on top. If the guessing is going slowly, let him put both hands in the box.

Some household objects that might become mystery items: a feather; a cotton ball, a tiny stuffed animal, a wash cloth, a sock, etc.

Wind Down

Invite your child to stretch out, tummy down, on the floor, the sofa, or the grass. Tell him it is time for you to wind him down. While you are telling him this, turn an imaginary key in the middle of his back, then roll him over and turn the key in the middle of his chest.

Help him wind down with some simple stretches. Raise one leg 90°, with the other leg extended and stretch it against your body. Then do the other. Have your child reach his hand as far as he can over his head while stretching himself waaaay out. Then have him touch his right toe as close as he can to his left arm and reverse. These exercises should not hurt. Make sure your child only does what is relaxing and comfortable.

TONING TIP

Stretching is as good for wound-up parents as for kids. Why not develop a routine where you relax and stretch together?

Mail

Save the junk mail. Then one day, tell your child you have some mail just for him that he can open and "read." Let him have fun opening and exploring all these papers that you have avoided. Maybe he can become the family coupon collector.

Story Time

We have talked about reading stories, telling stories, taping stories, and writing stories in other chapters. But how can there be a quiet time chapter without talking about reading?

Perhaps, you would like to keep a few special books in their own box just for quiet times, books your child loves and is eager to hear. As your child gets older, you may want to have a whole book which you can read a little at a time to relax together. Five year olds may like a Shel Silverstein book or a Hans Christian Andersen fairy tale. Try Arnold Lobell's Frog and Toad books. Young children are often absorbed by nursery rhymes, Richard Scary, and Dr. Seuss.

_____ TITLES TIP _____

For more titles look for one of several books, *Read Aloud Handbook* [Trelease], *Best in Children's Literature* [U. of Chicago] or *For Reading Out Loud* [Kimmel and Segel] that help parents find the best books.

Picnic

When it is time for a time out, call "Picnic." Bring a thermos or capped mug of juice (perhaps another of coffee or tea for you) and some snacks and a mat or spread and go somewhere that you don't usually go. It can be the front lawn or the living room rug or the middle of your king-sized bed. Have a snack together. Your child may want to help you put together the snack and put everything into a basket.

Swinging

A neighbor with two energetic children insists that the most calming midday remedy she knows is swinging—not the playground kind but the porch variety. String a hammock in your backyard or basement or keep a two seater swinging bench hooked to a tree. Just sitting and swinging together seems to wind everyone down. There isn't anything else you have to do but cuddle.

16

Keeping Kids Busy
When You're Busy Too

You may be your child's favorite playmate, but there are many times during the day when your child must do without your company. It is important for children to learn to play independently and self-reliantly. Even the most social children must learn how to entertain themselves when company is not at hand.

In this chapter, as in earlier chapters, you'll find many activities that can happily absorb a child in solitary play. At first his attention span may be short, but as he gets older and becomes more proficient, these activities can absorb longer and longer blocks of time. If something doesn't take hold at one age, wait a few months and try again.

Many of these activities can be repeated and expanded to fit the needs of older children.

Sharpshooter

Place a box or carton outside. Have your son arrange some objects on top of the box, side by side, or stacked in a pyramid. You can use plastic toys, blocks, or anything unbreakable.

Give your child a ball or a bean bag and an invitation to knock down the objects. Start your child off about two feet from the targets, and leave him to increase the distance from the box as skill and strength increase.

Bull's-Eye

With tape or chalk, mark two or three very large letters or numbers on an outside windowless wall. Using a ball, your child tries to hit each target.

An older child might use a tennis racquet or paddle and ball or even a bat and ball to hit the targets.

Water Works

Absolute absorption for most toddlers is a safe stool pulled up in front of a sink. All that's needed are different kinds and sizes of plastic bottles of different sizes, a funnel if you have one, and some margarine dishes or plastic measuring cups and spoons—a basting tube is pretty good, too—and water. Dozens of parents have told of us how terrific this is for absorbing little children for long periods of time.

A utility room sink or a bathroom with no carpet is perfect. Station yourself nearby and expect some quiet time of your own.

Make a Mural

Set your child to making a letters and numbers mural. He can make it just for fun or, if the occasion presents itself, as a gift for a younger child. Young children always feel important when they have a chance to be the "older" one and instruct an even younger child.

Provide a large sheet of paper—a very long sheet from an inexpensive roll of shelf paper works very well for this activity. The child must fill the sheet with letters and numbers, lots of letters and numbers, all the ones he can think of, in different sizes and shapes and colors. He may print them with crayons or paints, cut them out of magazines and paste them, trace them, or draw them on different kinds of paper and paste them on. He might want to do a border around the mural of letters and/or numbers.

Lacing Patterns

Give your child a hole puncher and let him punch holes all over a sheet of cardboard or heavy paper. Using a long shoelace or a string of heavy yarn that is knotted at one end, your child can have fun weaving through the holes, zigzagging in and out of the paper. Help him tie a knot in the loose end of the string when he is finished.

Several different colors of yarn make the end result even more fun. Another variation is to let your child bind together a collection of his artwork by punching holes along the left-hand margin and sewing the pages together.

TIP TIP

To avoid fraying on the tip of the yarn, wrap a piece of transparent tape around the end of the string, being careful not to overlap too much so it will not get too fat. This will give you a pointed tip, more like a shoelace, which will be easier to handle.

I'm an Author

Children love to make their own books. While you are busy with your own paperwork, let your child make a book. You can start with blank pages and sew or staple them together later, or you can begin by stapling the pages together, putting a number on each, and letting your child fill in the pages with one picture on each page.

The pages can be pictures he draws or pictures cut out from magazines. Like the children's books in the store, he can make books on different subjects—on animals, food, sports, or flowers. He might make books of different sizes—a BIG book, a medium book, or a small one. He can make his own TV guide with pictures of his favorite shows and a place to write in the time and station. Later on, when each of you is finished working, you can print text in the book as your child dictates.

Tissue Art

An absorbing art activity for children requires only a couple of boxes of different-colored tissues, glue, and some drawing paper. First your child tears a few tissues of each color into small pieces, crumples them, and sets them on a table, piled by color. Then he applies small dabs of paste here and there on the drawing paper. He attaches one end of a piece of crumpled tissue to each dab of paste. The tissue will adhere to that spot, while the remainder will appear puffy.

Once this technique is mastered, your child is set to take the abstract-art world by storm or to create all kinds of special effects on his own drawings; clouds, flowers, snowmen, and fire can all spring into three dimensions with tissues.

Sheet Retreat

"Kids like to go where grownups don't," Susan's son reminded us. And, to their great credit, they are not fussy. If you have a hall with many doors, close all the doors, pull out some sheets and tie them to the doorknobs with rubber bands. You will be creating some sort of unstructured tent city. Your child will likely be delighted to crawl under the sheets with his favorite toys and entertain himself happily.

Lemonade Stand

A favorite thing for children to do is set up a lemonade stand. Your child will probably need a companion or two for this. It is a good way for older and younger children to work together.

Remind the children they will need a wagon, a table, or a box from which to sell or give away their lemonade. They may want to decorate their cart or table first and make a sign. After they have gathered cups, drink, and perhaps ice, they are ready to set up a stand. You may suggest that very young children sell their drinks for only a few pennies. Older children can think more competitively about real costs. With them, you might suggest they pay a certain percentage of each sale for the supplies you are providing.

DIVERSIFICATION

Older children may add on or substitute for the lemonade business a face-painting stand for young neighbors—and daring adults. This will take a table, two chairs, a mirror, Vaseline or cold cream, and tissues. For painting, use eye shadow, eye liner, blush, and lipstick.

Car Wash

On a warm day, a great way for a young child to pass the time happily is to set him to work washing your car. You must, of course, not care too much what the car looks like afterward, unless you yourself are willing to get involved in this project.

Give your child a bucket of soapy water, several rags or large sponges, and a hose turned low. First, he can wash the car down. Then he can rinse the car and shine it with the rags.

Scrub Down

If you are not willing to turn your car over to your child or the weather is too cold, settle your child at the kitchen sink or with a large bucket instead, and let him scrub down his plastic and rubber toys. Put just a little detergent in the water and provide an old toothbrush for scrubbing.

Designer Dreams

Find an old, plain colored bottom sheet that fits your child's bed. Grab a handful of indelible magic markers and your child is ready for a great KIDFUN project. Let her decorate her sheet however she likes—she can do a self-portrait of herself sleeping, a jungle scene or anything else that strikes her fancy. How about covering the sheet with her name or with letters from the alphabet.

On other days, she can do a matching pillow case or top sheet.

Banker

This activity may launch your child on the road to high finance. Short of that, it will keep him occupied for quite a while. Help him empty the contents of his piggy bank on a table or the floor or a bed.

Now he can chart all his money. Leave him with a sheet divided into four columns, with a penny, a nickel, a dime, and a quarter taped at the top of each column (or he can make a rubbing of each coin). He can make a mark on the sheet for each coin or, if there are lots of them, sort them into piles of five and make a mark for each pile. Your child may not know how much money he has, but he will see that the biggest number of piles matches the column with the most marks.

Self-Portrait

Find some paper large enough for your child to lie down on. A wide roll of shelf paper or brown kraft paper works well. (In a pinch, you can tape together sheets of newspaper, but this is not as good as plain paper and works well only if your child has magic markers for coloring.) Draw your child's outline with a heavy black marker or crayon. That is your part. Now leave your child to consult the mirror to produce a life-size self-portrait, including clothing, jewelry, hair, and face.

For variation, she can draw only her face portrait by setting a mirror on her worktable and drawing herself as she looks at it.

Bag Puppets

Small brown lunch bags are easily transformed by young children into puppets. When the bag is folded flat, the bag bottom overlaps one side of the bag. Slide your hand inside the bag with your fingers around this bottom fold and make the fold open and shut like a mouth. Show your child this trick and then set him to work making his own puppet characters and puppet play to show you when you are done with your own tasks.

TIMELY TIP

When you and your child are working on individual projects, set a timer and tell your child you will be ready to take a break when the timer goes off.

Sandwich Vendor

Give your child sheets of construction paper in many colors. Also give her a five-inch-square pattern to cut squares from the paper. Now she can have fun putting them together as different sandwiches and making a pretend luncheonette.

For example, a square of brown and a square of purple between two squares of white make a peanut butter and jelly sandwich. Ham and cheese on whole wheat, egg salad on brown bread, and a hamburger (made from a circle of brown paper) with lettuce and tomato might all be served up. Your child will probably use her own imagination once you have started her off.

Tape Art

Buy a few rolls of different-colored tapes. All you need to do is give your child the tapes and some paper, and she is likely to take off without needing many directions. Children enjoy tearing the tapes into different sizes and lengths and crossing the colors into designs.

TINY TOTS TIP

If you cut the tape into strips of different lengths and let them dangle from the edge of the table, even a very young child can enjoy this activity and leave little mess.

Mock Smock

Surrender up a large, old shirt that your child can use as an art and cooking smock or a scientist's lab coat. Let her decorate the smock with iron-on transfers, indelible markers or embroidery thread. Don't have her do the whole smock at one time. One busy day, let her work on a sleeve. Another day she can choose another portion of the shirt.

PATCH PITCH

Slightly older children who have gotten interested in collecting patches from outings and trips can sew patches onto their smock. In this case, make sure you start with a big enough shirt so there is plenty of room to keep growing.

Monogram

What is it about personalized belongings that is appealing to people of all ages? If your child already has the coordination to sew, she might enjoy monogramming her own clothes. Start with a night shirt or T-shirt or, perhaps, a bath towel.

You can write the monogram on the cloth with a pencil—or she can monogram her first name. Let her pick the color thread. Encourage her to make very small stitches. That way, the monogram will look better, last longer and give you more time to get your work done.

MINIGRAM

For younger children, use letter stickers that come from office supply stores.

Tube Time

If you are already into recycling cans, bottles and newspapers, it may not take much effort to recycle the cardboard rolls from toilet paper and paper towels. Save them for a day when you need your child to be quietly absorbed and then bring out the whole bag, along with a role of masking tape and let your child construct her most elaborate tube sculptures.

TAPE TIP

If it is hard for your child to cut the tape herself, cut lots of pieces of varying lengths and tape them to the edge of the table for quick access.

Groovy Movie

What parent who owns both a television and a child has not put one in front of the other in search of some quiet time? Of course, television is not as good as Mary Poppins but since it is much more available, most of us use it in a crunch. However, instead of having your child settle for whatever is on at the moment, develop a collection of taped children's shows and movies that are content and age appropriate and let your child be glued to something worth watching.

A Short Sort

A couple times each year encourage your school-aged child to take an hour and sort through her belongings for what she has outgrown in mind or body.

Let your child know that toys and clothes that are in good condition are much needed by families who are having hard times just now and cannot buy new items. When you are busy but she is not, ask your child to look through her belongings for stuff she doesn't use or wear anymore.

Perhaps, together, you can from time to time, take these items to a center that distributes them. If you prefer, you can collect these items, along with those from other family members, for an annual yard sale. Maybe you want to let your children keep the money that is earned from the sale of their items to save, to spend, or to give to a special charity.

TOY TRADE

An alternative to selling is trading. A group of friends may like trading toys, books, and/or clothes for a few weeks at a time. Just make sure you don't put anything up for trade that you would feel really bad about never seeing again.

17

KIDFUN Gifts

L et your gift giving reflect the KIDFUN spirit. When it is time to give your children gifts for birthdays and holidays, choose gifts that will stimulate their imagination and reinforce their interest in active—and interactive—play.

Of course your child will want toys, especially those he or she has seen advertised on television. But experienced parents know that all too often these toys hold a child's interest for only a few days, and they are soon "lost" under the bed, in the bottom of the closet, or in the yard.

The best toys are those that are not limited to one set of instructions but can be used in a variety of ways and at a variety of ages. Our own favorite store-bought toys are a good, sturdy set of well-sanded wood blocks in various sizes and shapes, and other building modules. (Just make sure you don't buy very young children anything with pieces they can put into their mouths and swallow or into their ears or noses.)

Having invested in these staples of inventive play, parents are often perplexed about what to buy for the child whose toy chest looks like an advertisement for a toy store or who is bored with "baby toys" but not quite ready for the next stage of store-bought items. Kids have the most fun with real things, things that they can use again and again in useful and productive ways. Watch the pleasure a small child has sweeping the floor with a real, scaled-down broom, vacuuming the carpet with a small sweeper, or working at a bench with actual tools.

In this chapter you'll find a variety of innovative—and often quite inexpensive—solutions to the "What on earth can I buy?" dilemma. Most of these gifts reinforce activities in *The KIDFUN® Activity Book* and provide an organized resource kit for interactions with your children. And they make great gifts for your own children to take to birthday parties.

Instead of the toy store, we direct your attention to the hardware store, the office supply store, the crafts store, and the local pharmacy or five-and-ten. Another good place to shop is a school supply store for teachers.

Many of these gift ideas are make-it-yourself kits. You can make the kit as elaborate or as simple as your budget and your inclination allow. Use a cigar box or a cardboard shoe box or buy a plastic box, a cheerful lunch box, or a sectioned knick-knacks box at one of those containers stores that seem to be springing up in malls everywhere. You can have the box as plain or as fancy as you like—or make decorating the box a shared activity for later. And you can fill the box immediately—or you can make it a starter box and have the fun of adding surprise gifts from time to time.

Arts and Crafts Kit

Many of the activities that young children enjoy are arts and crafts projects. And having fresh, new supplies is a treat for both kids and adults.

An advantage of this gift is that you can put it together almost anywhere—in the supermarket, the drugstore, the office supply warehouse.

Into your box put any combination of the following:

colored paper, fat magic markers, skinny magic markers, crayons—also fat and skinny, colored pencils, chalk, colored tissue paper, glue, scissors, a ruler, a stencil, stickers, stars, and glitter. Don't forget to consider a fresh box of watercolor squares, some extra paintbrushes, carbon paper, a fat eraser, and poster board on the side.

If you go browsing in a crafts shop, the list becomes much longer still. There are beads of various shapes and sizes, wooden figures to paint, pastels, and special papers. You may want to buy one of the ready-made kits—for wreaths and candles and trains and houses. Talk to the salesperson, and find out just how difficult a kit can be. If the project is too hard, your child—and perhaps you—will become frustrated. Start with the basics. You can always add next year.

MOLDED MOMENTS

Many young children are delighted with painting plaster of Paris molds. These are inexpensive and come in all sorts of shapes—Indians, turtles, wreaths, Easter eggs, horses, and so on. Look under ceramics in the yellow pages or ask at the hobby shop.

Sewing Kit

Instead of a box, you might want to make this one a basket, with each item wrapped individually to add to the mystery. Put in a small pair of child-safe scissors, a collection of bright fabric squares, a handful of pretty buttons, a cardboard of ric-rac and one of lace, and, of course, needles, thread, and a thimble. Thread a few of the needles and tie a knot at the end so the thread will not slip away—and neither will your child's interest if you are not there to help thread a needle one rainy day. Put in an IOU for one hour of your time to teach her some sewing techniques. A good first project for a young lady might be a doll quilt.

Not only will you have an inexpensive and unique present, you will also have the makings of a lifetime of pleasure in a skill well learned. And don't forget that, in this age, boys need to know how to sew buttons and tears too.

A STITCH IN TIME

If you have a child who already enjoys sewing and has a sewing basket, introduce her to embroidery with hoops, a preprinted pattern, and some embroidery thread. Perhaps you can introduce her to knitting or crocheting. If your child enjoys these activities but you don't, think about a few hours of child swapping with a friend. Perhaps you can teach her son how to bake the world's best brownies while she introduces your daughter to the basics of embroidery.

Bag of Balls

The only suitable wrapping for this gift is a trash bag or a pillow case. Fill one or the other with all kinds of ball—rubber balls, tennis balls, beach balls, ping pong balls and a soccer ball, softball and basketball. You might want to write the child's name in fancy script on each ball. Matched with the right young athlete, this gift should roll out a big thanks.

BAG IT

Add to this gift by supplying an inexpensive athletic bag for storage.

Stickers, Stickers, Stickers

Stickers go in and out of fashion, but not in and out of fun. A boxful of stickers, with a small photo album for storing the collection, will delight children of many ages.

As you wander through your errands, keep an eye out for stickers. You will find them in a wide array of stores and in all sorts of sizes and shapes, sold individually on long rolls of paper or in packets with several pages to a packet. Buy them as you see them and tuck them away for the right gift-giving moment. And if you don't seem to see any, try an educational supply house or a large pharmacy or a party store.

Young children like stars and hearts and cartoon characters and funny faces. Older children are often delighted with stickers that have messages: "Awesome," "You're the best," and "Stick close to me." Add some plain postcards to the package, and your child can "write" letters with the stickers to family and friends.

Face Painting Kit

Here is a wonderful gift that can stretch your child's imagination, set her up in the face-painting business, or just send you and her and her friends into a serious state of the giggles. From the drugstore, buy a few nonallergenic cosmetics: blush, powder, eye shadow colors, and lipstick. Add an inexpensive lipstick brush, an eyebrow pencil, and perhaps a small stand-up mirror. Be sure to include a jar of cold cream and a box of tissues. Both girls and boys will have a wonderful time experimenting with this stuff. As part of the present, let your child make you up, too.

_____ FANCY LADIES _____

For little girls who love to pretend they are mom or big sister putting on makeup, make this a makeup kit for a big-little girl. Add a bit of nail polish and a splash of child's cologne.

A variation on this theme is a manicure kit for a young miss, complete with emery board, polish, polish remover, and cotton balls. Add a piece of plastic for protecting the table.

Theater Props

Supplement your child's imagination with a big box of props. There are a few staples that make a perfect starter kit for family theatrics: a black cape, a wig, a cane, a high hat, and a pair of glasses with a phony nose. Kids love clown paraphernalia, too. Look for big plastic shoes, rubber noses, large ties, and silly hats. Clown makeup is an extra bonus.

Halloween time is the easiest time to fill your props box, but during the rest of the year look in costume shops or theater prop shops.

Vintage Wear

An unusual but fruitful place to shop for a birthday or holiday gift is the local thrift shop.

From second-hand stores you can put together a tempting collection of dress-up items that will allow a young miss to sweep and swoop around the living room for you. She might even organize a backyard fashion show with her friends for parents. Look for hats—with feathers and veils and great big brims. Check out the clothes racks for anything velvet, large shawls, and a bright, silky blouse. Shop the formal rack for something in tulle or taffeta that fell on hard times and is suitably cheap but still has enough rustle to delight a young miss. If you're lucky, you might find a long white bridal veil. Look, too, for a pair of glitzy high heels, long chains, and a big purse.

A wonderful way to package this present is in one of those large cardboard storage boxes you can buy inexpensively.

For boys, head for the hats. Bowlers and canes and wide, wide ties are perfect. Look, too, for military gear, tuxedos, and sportsman vests with all kinds of pockets.

If this gift is a success, you can add to the collection on different occasions and have your own prop room for instant, impromptu dress-up. You should get into the spirit and dress up too.

GERM BRIGADE

Examine the dress-up items you buy carefully to see that nothing is in the pockets and that they are suitably clean.

Water Fun

If you are heading toward summer and, even better, toward the beach, a bucket of water toys is a grand gift. But all you really need to make this work is a backyard with a hose and a small sandbox.

Don't fool around with kids' buckets with flimsy handles. Go directly to the hardware or discount store and get a sturdy kitchen bucket. Into it goes a collection of nonbreakable bottles, plastic cups, a baster, some cookie cutters, a sifter, and perhaps a water gun. Tie a big red bow on the handle and you are ready to delight your toddler. (And come winter and snowy days, many of the same toys will be useful.)

A watering can, a plastic wading pool, tubes or water wings, a beach ball, goggles, flippers, and outdoor games are additions to your water fun list of gifts.

INSTANT SAND

If you have the hose but not the sand, think about a sandbox for a gift. Four pieces of treated wood for the sides and several bags of high-grade sand will get you by. Put your bucket and bow in the middle of the sand pile and surprise your child one birthday morning. Add some sand "toys,"—a metal spatula for flattening, a soup ladle for shoveling, an ice cream scoop for working perfectly with wet sand.

Serious Business

We might want to escape the trappings of our workaday world, but many children find the paraphernalia of work just right for having fun.

When Sharla's children were young, they loved to set up store in their toy closet and spend long afternoons preparing their toys for sale and then "selling" them to each other and their friends. All it took to get them started was a supply of paper money, a bunch of small sales tags, a date and price stamp, and an ink pad from the local office supply store.

Walk the aisles of a well-stocked office supply store, and you will find all sorts of things to tweak a youngster's interest: bunches of colored rubber bands, magnets, small carbonized pads to play waiter with while serving gourmet play dough to the stuffed animal crowd (or just plain carbon for a young artist's experiments), different kinds of stamps and ink pads, rolls of colored tapes and ledger books for children who like to tally up money or baseball cards or other collectibles.

Think about buying an inexpensive Rolodex for a small child. Add a few special numbers neatly printed with personal drawings so the child will know which number is Grandma's, which is your office, and which is the policeman. As your children get older—and spend more time on the phone—they will like having their own Rolodex for friends' numbers, too, especially if the school phone book vanishes as frequently in your house as in ours.

Older children will be pleased to own their own stapler, hole puncher, and big tape dispenser. You may be pleased not to have to share yours.

Name It

A personalized stamp is a great gift. They come in all sizes and styles and can be ordered at stationery or office supply stores and often at private postal stores. Add ink pads in three different colors. Then one rainy day, you can put your child to work stamping her name in all her books.

Personalizing has become big business, and you may want to consider paper pads, carved wooden signs, stickers, or pens with your child's name.

Stationery

Plan ahead and give your child a gift of personalized paper. There is something about having our name in print that delights people of all ages. Just as colleagues at work enjoy having note pads or a letterhead with *their* name at the top, children too get a sense of pride and importance in having their name in print.

You can order stationery, postcards, tablets, calling cards for gift enclosures, or even "business cards" that have your child's name and address and phone and a bit of personal art. Your child can use these with new friends whom she would like to encourage to call.

KIDOGRAMS

If your child is really taken with her name in print, you can splash it on towels, sheets, place mats, toothbrushes, barrettes. We have also seen in catalogues cups and plates, key rings, brass name plates, and picture frames that can be personalized. Or buy the squeeze tubes of permanent paint or indelible markers and let your child personalize her own sheets, T-shirts, or towel.

High-Tech

In keeping with our experience that kids like "real" things and that real things often last longer than toy imitations, shop the electronics department for children's gifts. Even a four-year-old can enjoy her own tape recorder and with it her own collection of stories and music. Ask a librarian at school or in the children's room of the public library for suggestions of what to buy. There are many tapes now just for kids.

As children get a little older, they will be delighted to receive a Walkman—but remember that putting a young head between two earphones prevents, instead of promotes, interaction. You might want to set some boundaries for when and where Walkman listening is acceptable.

For a child going off to school for the first time, her own clock radio or alarm clock is an important gift. She will feel very grown-up to have her own clock, and you can start teaching her that waking up on time is her responsibility.

Hat Trick

For kids who like to dress up, think about a box of hats. A party supply store can provide all kinds of hats, from a cardboard top hat with glitter to a witches' peak. As you are making your rounds about town, look for odd hats—a straw panama, a paper chef's hat, a sombrero. Collect them and hide them away until you have a box full.

Athletics

The sporting goods store is another place to find a gift that you and your child can enjoy together. (Just don't forget—this is not YOUR gift, it is your child's gift.) High-pressuring a child into the sport of your choice is more likely to result in aversion than a trip to the Olympics. But if you are relaxed and low key, and emphasize having fun over perfecting skills, sports are a perfect place for parents and children to find common pleasure.

Treat your child to a simple fishing rod and let it be the impetus for a fishing trip. Any kind of ball—basketball, football, softball, tennis ball, beach ball—is a consideration. Bats and mitts and golf clubs and tennis racquets are all traditional favorites—for girls as well as boys. But think also about badminton, croquet, and volleyball, easily adapted to backyard play.

School-age children may be delighted to own binoculars—add a book about birds—or a sports bag for hauling gym stuff—add a lock with the kind of combination you can set to suit yourself.

One of our personal best sporting-goods-store successes was a small, soft stand-up punching bag that provided a perfect outlet for feisty aggressions.

PENNYSAVER

Young children often want sports equipment like that of their older siblings but are not mature enough to use and care for expensive items properly. Satisfy their need with second-hand equipment until they are ready to move up. We have wonderful memories of a neighborhood two-year-old who carried his used squash racquet everywhere, asking "Tennith anyone?"

Hobby Helpers

It is hard to predict when a gift will capture a child's attention in a really powerful way and open that child to long-term investigation—but when it happens, when a young child "takes" to a particular gift and uncovers a passion for painting or kites or puzzles, for stamps or knitting or building models, for making jewelry or decorating cakes or tooling leather or keeping bees, that gift is worth its proverbial weight in gold. We know children who are mesmerized by making stained-glass objects, decorating T-shirts, braiding belts, and stringing beads, and others who will spend hours on submarine ship models, model trains, or dollhouses. And we also know children who have no interest in long-term hobbies, no interest in fiddling with any of these ideas, and no need for anything more than a blue sky and an open field.

Look for gifts that have the potential for growing into hobbies. Take into account the temperament of the particular child. Think about whether this child likes best to be indoors or outdoors, using large or small motor skills, working patiently with details or getting results quickly.

Working with a child on his or her hobby can be a special bond between the two of you. If you have a favorite hobby and the child can come to share it, that is terrific opportunity for KIDFUN. But sometimes a child's interests are different from those of her parents. In this case, an aunt or uncle, grandparent, older cousin, or neighbor may be the perfect person to share a hobby.

We may be tempted to rush our children into activities because we are so eager to expose them to new things, so delighted with the idea of working together with our child—even when they are not quite ready for the introduction. If a gift just sits and your child shows no interest, tuck it away in a closet and leave it there for a year or two. What flops at five may be a take at seven.

There is, of course, no easy formula for knowing when a child is "ready," but try looking for other children who are engaged in the hobby you have in mind. See what age they are, and ask them at what age they first became interested. Make sure your child has a sufficient attention span and motor skills for the activity you have in mind.

Tool Kit

A longtime favorite toy of very young children is a "workbench" of pegs and a wooden mallet to pound the pegs in and out of the bench's holes. When your child is ready to move on, think about introducing her to real tools. Buy her an inexpensive tool kit and fill it with starter tools. Our own experience is that the tools in the hardware store last longer and are better buys than the tools designed especially for children.

Start with a lightweight hammer, a tape measure, and a screw driver. Add an assortment of large nails and some pieces of wood. To this you can add a leveler, a clamp, a pair of pliers, and a work apron with pockets as well.

Then pick a simple project and work with your child. You and your child might try small bookcases, toy boxes, and three-hook clothes bars for the back of the bathroom door for starters.

Flashlights

Light up some youngster's life with a flashlight—or a collection of flashlights. Little kids, especially, seem delighted with the magic of flashlights.

These come now in all sizes, shapes, and prices. You might want to buy a poppa-size, a momma-size, and a baby-size light, wrap each separately, and drop them in a brightly colored shopping bag. Don't forget to include the right-size batteries for each light—and to take some time after the excitement of gift getting wears off to explain just how batteries work: A light left burning under the bed will not last very long.

Linens for Little People

It may seem funny to shop for little people in the linen department, but we found one of our children's most adored gifts there. Ours was a soft, red sleeping bag with cartoon characters on the front, and it was used on the bed, in the family room, under the dining-room table, and in the backyard tent until it was more holes than cloth. Kids also like sheets and pillow cases that are fun and beach towels with favorite characters or bold and bright designs. These are a particularly good gift when you need to send a present to a child you don't know very well.

Kidman

Find an inexpensive "walkman" with only a tape cassette player. Add to it a collection of children's songs on tape. Little kids love having their very own headphones and tapes. (The reason we prefer no radio is to keep your child from plugging in and tuning out.)

Computer Stuff

In the five years between this expanded edition and the first edition of *The KIDFUN® Activity Book*, educational software for young children has grown enormously with new products coming out all the time. We have come to believe that the computer can, indeed, be a good source of KIDFUN.

Many of the new products, even for very young children, build critical thinking and imagination. Kids think they are fun, and adults get hooked, too. If you have a home computer, get familiar with some of the products by reading about them or inquiring. You will probably get better information in one of the newer stores springing up to serve parents interested in educational toys and computer software than in a general computer store.

We have only one caution. Make time on the computer a cheerful activity, a reward not a mandatory practice. It is not important that your young child master level one and keep moving on in record time. You want your child to see the computer as a friend and a helpful tool, not as task that must be addressed. Even high tech can be KIDFUN.

KIDFUN Certificate

Here is a gift especially well suited to your nieces or nephews or godchildren. Give yourself for an afternoon with the promise to take the child to a place of her choice—a movie, a fast food lunch, or a trip to the zoo, the museum, or the beach. Include a few dollars for spending money inside a card with a KIDFUN certificate—or buy a sheet of poster board and make a really large certificate.

Family Favorites

We can get so involved keeping up with the newest video games and electronic extravaganzas that we forget about the traditional gift-giving staples that have served generations of children.

A deck of cards holds hours of fun. So does a jigsaw puzzle, a coloring book, and a rolling pin for kitchen cooking. What child wouldn't love a wonderful book to read aloud and an old-fashioned board game that has been tested by several generations of children? A bag of jacks, a can of pick-up sticks, a box of tiny cars, or a jar of bubbles for each of you are nearly foolproof gifts. Children don't measure gifts by how much they cost but rather by how much fun they are to use—and use again. And if you and your child can use them together, they are a real investment for the future.

In Closing

THINK BACK

Think back to your own childhood. How many memories are of giggles? How many recollections focus on fun and laughter?

The number-one goal of this book is to give parents and kids more good times and more good-time memories. The pace of contemporary life makes stress a prevalent condition and irritation a commonplace emotion. But stress and irritation are not the stuff of which happy childhoods are made. And happy kids make a better world.

LEMONS TO LEMONADE

The aim in writing KIDFUN was to help parents and grandparents and other caretakers make the most of the moments that we have with our children. And, for us, "make the most" does not mean make the most educational progress. Many of the activities in this book have a learning component and are developmentally helpful for young children, but the focus is not on making smarter, brighter, more precocious kids. It is on taking times that could go sour—traffic jams, supermarket lines, rainy weeks, sick days—and turning them into opportunities for a happy time together.

Now the majority of preschool as well as elementary school children have no stay-at-home parent. Time is a scarce commodity. Fatigue is much less scarce. Our children are as likely to see us in the car, the supermarket, the office, or the waiting room as in the backyard. KIDFUN is designed to recognize these realities and turn them to a child's advantage.

GIVE YOU TO YOUR CHILDREN

In this busy world, stop and smell the roses. Give YOU to your children. They will be forever grateful. Take the times you are given to parent, whether planned or unplanned, and make the most of them. In retrospect, childhood goes quickly—even when certain weeks seem dreadfully long. We hope, from the perspective of hindsight, you will be able to look back and say, "I made the most of it!"

KIDFUN Shopping List

Most activities in this book require only a willing spirit and a waiting child. The whole purpose of *The KIDFUN® Activity Book* is to present ways to seize the moment wherever and whenever it occurs. When supplies are required, they are mostly items easily found in households with children—pillows, sponges, children's toys. But, of course, the day you want to do something with straws or Cheerios, there will be none in the house.

For your convenience, here is an advance-planning shopping list of activity "ingredients" that you might not have at hand and would like to keep in a KIDFUN drawer:

From the Supermarket

Alka Seltzer
bags, lunch bag sized
balloons
basting tube
beans, dried
bubbles
cassette tapes
Cheerios or other cereal in similar shape
construction paper
cookie cutters

elastic
flashlight and batteries
food coloring
Jello and pudding mixes
M&Ms or similar candy
markers, colored ones and an indelible laundry pen
miniature marshmallows
paper plates and cups
pastas in a variety of small shapes including alphabet letters
pencils, colored
plastic bottles and bowls in various shapes
popsicle sticks
Post-it notes
rolling pin
rope
shelf paper, roll of the widest plain paper
sponges, thin
strainer
straws, preferably plastic
string
terry towels
tongs

Office or Art Supplies

(Some of these things will be found in many supermarkets as well.)

carbon paper
chalk—both regular and fat sizes
clay
erasers
felt
foam in various shapes

glue, white liquid
lick-on stars
magnets
needles—plastic embroidery with slip-in eye and
    sewing needles with large eyes
paint brushes in assorted sizes
paste
poster board
restaurant order books
rub-off letters
rubber bands
stamp with child's name and ink pad
tempera paints
tissue paper
yarn

Special Household Items

accordion folders
beach equipment
card games for kids
cookie sheet, plastic
hole punch
hula hoop
kites
lawn sprinkler (we like the circle ones)
mirror, non-breakable
rake, child-sized
tape recorder
tennis balls
U.S. map
water pistol
wigs and hats

Index

Entries shown in **boldface** are activity titles.